YOU ME HE

Sex really isn't a dirty word!

by Sammy Tippit
as told to Jerry Jenkins

This book is designed for your personal reading pleasure and profit. It is also designed for group study. A leader's guide, with visual aids (SonPower Multiuse Transparency Masters) is available from your local Christian bookstore or from the publisher.

VICTOR BOOKS

a division of SP Publications, Inc.
WHEATON ILLINOIS 60187

Offices also in Fullerton. California • Whitby. Ontario. Canada • Amersham-on-the-Hill. Bucks. England

Third printing, 1980

Bible quotations are from the *New American Standard Bible* (NASB), © 1960, 1962, 1963, 1968, 1971, 1972, 1973, 1975, The Lockman Foundation, La Habra, California. Other quotations are from the *New International Version* (NIV), copyright © 1973 by New York Bible Society International.

Library of Congress Catalog Card Number: 77-95030
ISBN: 0-88207-766-X

VICTOR BOOKS
A division of SP Publications, Inc.
P.O. Box 1825 • Wheaton, Ill. 60187

YOU ME **HE**

To our wives, of course:
Debra Ann Sirman (Tex) Tippit
and
Dianna Louise Whiteford Jenkins

Contents

The Authors

Sammy Tippit, 30, is an international speaker and evangelist who specializes in working with young people. He heads God's Love in Action, Inc., P.O. Box 27175, San Antonio, TX. The ministry's work has taken him all over the United States and to several Iron Curtain countries.

Jerry Jenkins, 28, is managing editor of *Moody Monthly* magazine and is the author of 14 books, four published by Victor Books. He wrote *God's Love in Action* (Broadman Press and Moody Press) and *Three Behind the Curtain* (Whitaker House), both with Sammy Tippit.

Introduction

The basic principles from Scripture and from life presented here for Christians may make you think, *Man, you've got to be kidding. This is too straight. It's too hard!* I've simply tried to present a biblical standard that should be lifted high in a world that has no standards.

You may not agree with everything, but as you look toward setting a biblical standard for dating, seek your own answers in God's Word — the Bible. God will guide you if you honestly seek His answers to your questions. He may deal differently with different people, but He *never* violates His own Laws.

Apply God's guidance, and you will have a successful dating life. I pray that you will diligently consider the stake God has in your love life, and that you will build your life—whether married or single—around the Word of God. May your life be as beautiful and fulfilling as God intended it to be. God bless you.

Sammy Tippit

1 God's Standard for Dating

"I'll not allow my children to hear this!" the mother of two teenage daughters almost screamed. "These things should be talked about at home, not at church!" Pushing her daughters up the aisle in front of her, the woman stomped from the church building. I was devastated.

In speaking about God's standard for dating, I found myself telling it to the kids pretty straight. I challenged young people to make a radical commitment to Jesus Christ and to build their lives around Him.

Being just over 21 years old at the time, I knew that young people weren't as naive as they were just a generation ago. So I was telling them precisely how they needed to let God control their minds and bodies.

I felt I had been careful and tactful, though direct, with this group of young people in a southern Louisiana church. I thought the young people had been hungry for some straight talk. Had I been wrong?

The lady's actions shook me so badly I didn't

know what to do. I stood speechless for seconds that seemed like minutes. Before I could collect my thoughts the woman burst back in, pleading with other parents: "Take your children out of here!"

No one moved. "Let's bow our heads," I said, still flabbergasted. "God," I prayed, "if I was wrong in sharing your standards so straight and directly tonight, I want You to forgive me —" I couldn't go on. I had felt God's presence throughout the evening, but this outburst had shaken my confidence. I broke down and wept, leaving the platform and going to a little room off to the side of the speaker's platform.

As I sat there praying and searching myself for any wrong motive, someone knocked at the door. It was the teen-aged son of the pastor. "Sammy," he said, with tears in his eyes, "I want to ask God for forgiveness." I stared at him in silence. "I have been sexually involved with one of the girls whose mother just made her leave the meeting. I know it's morally and biblically wrong and I need God's forgiveness." We prayed and he confessed his sin, asking God to forgive him.

After he left, there was another knock at the door. A young man I had been praying with all week said, "I've never heard anyone talk so straight to kids. I really want to know Jesus Christ."

After we prayed and he received Christ, yet another young person came to the door. Also in tears, this young girl said, "Sammy, I have only one regret about what you shared tonight. I wish you'd said it two months ago. I'm pregnant and not married."

Those three visitors confirmed that I'd been right in speaking from my heart about love, dating, and sex. I'm convinced that young people want it told straight and clear. What we hear about the subject from other-than-Christian sources is often grossly explicit, and out of context. The true and real and beautiful picture needs to be presented as well.

Reacting to the puritanical excesses of the past and the sexual liberation of the 60s, many parents and leaders have slipped into the dangerous assumption that young people already know all there is to know about sex and dating. There's no need for a Watergate-type whitewash; the message must get through. And soon.

Meanwhile, young people are often left to guess, to wonder, and to make their own romantic judgments. When people don't know God's standard, their social, sexual, and spiritual lives go to ruin.

The Standards

There are two sets of standards for *any* action in life, not just dating. The first is the world's, and the second is God's. The world's standard is based on "self." A person bases his conduct on what he wants, sees, knows, and thinks. He knows what he wants, sees it, justifies it, goes after it, and his life is destroyed. The Bible says, "There is a way which seems right to a man, but its end is the way of death" (Proverbs 14:12).

I can't count the number of people who have told me, "Everyone does it. It looks like fun. Besides, I'm not going to hurt myself or anyone else." But what has looked like fun has left bitterness, broken hearts, and shattered relationships.

Newsweek magazine reports that four of every ten new marriages in the U.S. end in divorce. These are often marriages based on faulty values. The husband may have married for sex. The wife for security. The world's philosophy, which often comes masqueraded in a costume of fun or security, can also end in death. This philosophy may be "my thing," but it's also a dead-end road of self-philosophy, self-value, and self-judgment.

God's standard does not end in death. It leads to life. Jesus said He came to give life and give it more abundantly. On the surface, the Christian life (especially in relation to dating and sex) may seem to be no fun, not fast-moving enough. But I know it can be a great joy to live for Christ—even on a date.

When I became a Christian I had just graduated from high school and was planning to enter Louisiana State University. I was being rushed by all the fraternities and had been to party after party for girls and booze and fun. When I received Christ, my whole value system changed. He became the center of my life, including my dating.

My friends thought I had gone crazy. They razzed me, saying I'd flipped out: "He prays with girls instead of trying to hustle them." But recently, when I attended the tenth anniversary reunion of my high school graduating class, I was saddened to see that many of those who had made fun of my values are now divorced—some of them twice. They had dated around, gone to wild parties, sowed their wild oats, and had their flings. Many of their marriages had gone bad and their happiness was a faded memory of a few good times.

Their own standards had given them nothing to base true love upon. My marriage is strong, built on the solid rock of God's standards, where Christ is central and my wife and I live for Him. Things aren't always perfect, but we know where to turn when we face rough times. Our happiness is not just a memory. It is now, and it will last forever.

How to Receive Christ*
For the benefit of any who have never clearly heard God's plan of salvation, a simple outline of this kind of Good News deserves careful study:

1. Man's Purpose
Man was created to be in union with God (Genesis 1:26-27), to be exulting in His glory and infinite life (John 17:3; 1 Peter 5:10).

---

*Adapted from *Anybody Here Know Right from Wrong?* by Bill Stearns, published by Victor Books, Wheaton, Ill. © 1972 SP Publications.

2. Man's Sin

The first man, Adam, decided to disobey, to reject, to step out on God (Romans 5:12). This cut Adam off from communion with the perfect God, and the sinful nature was passed down through the whole family of mankind. Without God, we're unable to fulfill our original purpose, and we feel empty.

3. Terrible News

Doing all kinds of good things doesn't wipe away sin in us. Finding out all we can about ourselves and about God doesn't do anything about being cut off from Him either. We remain miles away from being happily what God intended us to be. When we die we end up living an eternity away from our God (Hebrews 9:27; Romans 6:23).

All this is crummy: We were born with a sinful nature we didn't ask for, there's nothing we can do to get rid of that nature, and because of it we end up living an eternity in hell.

4. Great News: God

Yet God knew it would happen. He was willing to risk rejection when He gave us a choice to go His way or our own way. It was the only arrangement that could make devotion to Him realistic. (He *could* have created people as a company of dutiful robots proclaiming, "We-love-You-God! We-love-You-God!") But at the scene of the first sin (Genesis 3:15), God promised a Solution—a coming One who would buy mankind back from sin's grasp and who would crush sin's power

(Romans 5:6-8). So Jesus Christ came to take the results—the automatic penalties—of our sins. He experienced all our infinite hells for us by being separated from the Father on the bloody cross of Calvary (1 John 2:2).

5. More Great News: Jesus

That's great, right? But did you notice something? Since Jesus went through the hells each of us should have to go through, the individual person is united with God, right? Nope. Though "Christ died for the sins of the whole world" (1 John 2:2), if that's all there is to what He did for us, we're in the same old cut-off-from-God situation since we're still trapped in our sinful natures!

But Jesus didn't simply die and waste away in the grave like so many dead-end religious leaders. He brought Himself back from the dead! (2 Corinthians 5:15, 21) He's able—as Spirit—*to step into my life*. At my invitation, Jesus will come to live in me (Revelation 3:20). He will take control of my life and make me new (2 Peter 1:4).

God won't force His solution of salvation on us. We, like the first Adam, still have a choice of going God's way or our own. And our choice rests on Jesus Christ. Will we trust in the fact of His death which paid the penalty for our sins? Will we receive Him as the ruler of our lives—the One who is going to be our Life in God? (John 1:12) The Bible puts it this way: "If you confess with your mouth Jesus as Lord, and believe in your heart that God raised Him from the dead [after

He died especially for you], you shall be saved"
(Romans 10:9).

Make sense?

If you've never come to the definite point of
decision of receiving Christ, is there any good
reason not to do just that right now?

Based On The Word Of God

God's standards are clearly outlined in His Word,
the Bible. The Apostle Paul says that "all Scripture is inspired by God and profitable for teaching, for reproof, for correction, for training in
righteousness" (2 Timothy 3:16). No one likes to be
corrected or reproved. But there are only two al-
ternatives: When we play by God's rules, we
always win. Otherwise, we lose. And He has rules
for becoming the kind of people we should be,
relating to others, and showing us how to live
in marriage.

The man who led me to Christ, an evangelist
named James Robison, challenged me to center
my dating life around the Word of God. He
specified such things as avoiding lust of the flesh
and lust of the eyes, and attempting to honor each
other's bodies, putting them under God's control.
These ideas were radically different for me, but as
I read the Bible, I decided that I wanted to be
100% obedient to God.

Before anyone can discover God's standard and
live by it, he needs to believe two things. First, he
must come to the place where he decides that God
has a better idea for his life than he has himself.

Rarely will a person reject God's gift of Jesus Christ if he fully understands that Christ died for his sin. Jesus' death and His miraculous resurrection paved the way for bridging the great sin gap between God and man.

When you receive Christ as your Lord and become a Christian, you will also see that God's way is better than your own philosophy of life.

The person seeking God's standard must also have a growing faith in God's Word.

How can you know the joy God has for you in dating—or in any area of life—unless you trust that the Bible is His message to you? You may disagree with it; it may not add up to your philosophy of what makes sense or is logical. But unless you are willing to say, "God, I believe Your Word and I'm willing to obey it," you will be left to live on your own—based on the ways that seem right to you, but which end in death.

Not Just An Improvement

Our standards should not be minor improvements over what the world says is OK. Paul told the Christians at Rome, "I urge you therefore, brethren, by the mercies of God, to present your bodies a living and holy sacrifice, acceptable to God, which is your spiritual service of worship.

"Do not be conformed to this world, but be transformed by the renewing of your mind, that you may prove what the will of God is, that which is good and acceptable and perfect" (Romans 12:1-2).

This shoots holes in the arguments of those who say, "If everyone is doing it, it must be right." Maybe you haven't heard people say just those words, and maybe it sounds like a cliché to you, but how many people do you know who live as if "everyone's doing it" is justification for their actions?

We're not to be like this world. Just because everyone is going here, doing this, experiencing that is no reason to assume that it's right. But based on the Scripture just quoted, it's also a reason to assume that all that going, doing, and experiencing might be wrong.

Ironically, those who scream the loudest about nonconformity to standards usually conform to the standards of their peers. One of the most difficult pressures anyone, including adults, can face is peer pressure. By their very lives and dress and actions, friends can shout without voices that "you must follow or you will be left out!"

A lot of people cop out on true Christian standards for dating by protesting that they haven't engaged in the actual sex act, and thus elevate themselves a bit over "the world." But according to Paul's letter to the Christians at Rome, this is not enough. The key word isn't *improved* or a *little better;* the key is being *made new* by the renewing of the mind.

God's standard is found in the person of Jesus Christ. There are no shortcuts—no substitutes. To live right we must center our lives on Him. Somehow we've gotten the idea that Jesus is only relevant on Sundays or on certain holidays or in times of trouble. We pull Him out of our back pockets and wave Him around and say, "Here I am, everybody, Super Christian."

The following day, no one can tell we're Christians. We need to realize that Jesus is not someone we can pull out of our back pockets when we want to. Jesus Christ, living in us Christians, is here for eternity. We are letting Him in on anywhere we go, and anything we do, say, and think. Realizing this will radically change any Christian's standard of living, especially in the area of dating and sex.

The reason even a simple improvement over the world's standard isn't enough is because of the teaching of Jesus in the Beatitudes. There Christ says, "Blessed are the pure in heart, for they shall see God" (Matthew 5:8). To see God's will in our lives, we must follow His standard of purity of heart. It's not good enough to just do or not do certain things. Jesus went further than particular actions. He went straight to the heart—the motives.

Jesus gives a specific example: "You have heard that it was said, 'You shall not commit adultery'; but I say to you, that everyone who looks on a woman to lust for her has committed adultery with her already in his heart" (Matthew 5:27-28). We may be satisfied with an improvement over the loose morals of the world and think we are pure because we have not engaged in a specific sexual activity. But God's standard indicates that a person who has allowed Christ to be the center of his dating life, must also be pure in motive and intention.

If you're like me, having pure intentions means total dependence upon Christ. I'm human—I can't be pure. Perhaps with self-control, discipline, and hard work, I can maintain pure actions for a while. But only God, through Christ, can bring about that kind of purity in heart and mind.

Let's not be naive. We are not trying to pretend that we don't have normal sex drives. Guys and gals were beautifully created to be drawn to each other and to accomplish perfect marital unity as God intends. Our sex drive is a natural part of maturing, of being distinctly male or female. But that drive is controlled by God in those who give it to Him. It can be held in check until its proper, perfect time.

As love grows, the sex drive intensifies, making it even more important that a couple continually submit themselves to the power of Christ. Then a beautiful, pure, and holy union can take place, making the marriage godly. There will be no regrets, no skeletons in the closet, or no tearful confessions. Marriages of pure young people may be terribly rare today, but this should be the goal of every Christian who marries.

We all know of couples who seem to just coexist. They have little in common and never seem to grow closer together. The only time they are close is when they are in physical contact.

They may be kissing, French kissing, necking,

making out (the words change), or even engaged in intercourse, but otherwise they constantly bicker at each other. The longer they date, the more they argue. We wonder how they stay together—or maybe we don't wonder.

Theirs is a relationship based mainly on sexual experiences, however innocent or involved they may be. They will never have a lasting, meaningful relationship, let alone a loving one, because they are far from the standard that points to Christ. Their glue is sex, and when that is the center rather than a natural ingredient in its proper place and time, it loses its adhesiveness. The end is destruction.

2 God's Purpose for Dating

Becoming a Christian right at the time I began attending college made it a particularly exciting time for me. I really loved the Lord and wanted to share Him with others and glorify Him in everything I did. One of the first areas He worked on in me was my dating life. I wanted to be what He wanted me to be, especially in that area. But I didn't know how difficult that was.

Some of the things I did in my youth and newness in the Lord have been pretty dumb and I wouldn't recommend them as models for you. However, even in my ignorance, God took care of me and taught me in His grace and knowledge. One such incident resulted in God's glory, in spite of all my blundering.

I was going to speak at a youth gathering in a church on the other side of town on Saturday night when they had "date night." The young people of the church were encouraged to bring their dates to the meeting. Not being from that area, I asked a Christian friend to arrange a blind date for me.

When I called him for her name and address I was shocked to find that he had lined me up with a girl I'd dated before I was a Christian. "Oh, no!" I said, almost in shock. "What's she going to think when I ask her to pray with me and dedicate the date to the Lord? I have new standards for my dates, and she's gonna think I've flipped out!"

"That's your problem, Sam," he told me with a chuckle.

"You're a fine friend," I said.

We Christians are constantly engaged in spiritual warfare (Ephesians 6:10-18). I never felt it more acutely than while I was on the way to pick her up. The Lord was encouraging me to maintain my new standard of conduct on the date while Satan was assuring me that she'd think I was crazy.

I met her parents and escorted her to the car. When I slid behind the wheel, the Lord convicted me that I should pray and dedicate the date to Him. I was scared, and Satan was still urging me not to do it. I drove away in silence, but the battle raged on.

Finally I couldn't stand it any longer. I pulled into a high school parking lot and turned off the engine. She looked at me and scooted over close. I smiled sheepishly and said, "You're not going to believe this, but I want to pray and dedicate this date to Jesus. You see, since I saw you last, I've become a Christian. I want to glorify Christ on this date and in everything I do."

She was speechless, so I went ahead and prayed

briefly. When we arrived at the church, the pastor and the guy who had arranged the date were waiting for me to join them in a prayer meeting before the service. Another shocker for my date.

The meeting itself was informal and consisted mainly of Christians telling what the Lord meant to them and what He had done in their lives. My date sat silently during the invitation while other kids prayed to receive Christ. One of those who received Christ was the organist from my home church who had provided the special music that night. She said she'd been a phony for years and wanted to receive Christ as her Saviour.

After the meeting we went out with the organist and her boyfriend for pizza. She was bubbling over with joy and my date hardly knew what to make of it. The new Christian talked on and on about how she knew the Lord was real and how great it was. Her date was nodding and saying "Amen, that's right," and I kept exclaiming, "Wow, that's fantastic!"

My date stared incredulously at each of us. I wasn't sure how to approach the subject with her afterwards, so when I drove her home and walked her to the door, I said simply, "It's been great and we've had a good time. I'd like to thank God for it." I prayed and when I finished, tears were streaming down her face.

"Sammy," she said, "you really have changed. And I want to become a Christian too." We prayed together and she received Christ. Except for my dates with the girl who became my wife, that blind date turned out to be the most exciting one I ever had.

Paul wrote the people at Corinth: "Whether, then, you eat or drink or whatever you do, do all to the glory of God" (1 Corinthians 10:31). This means that the most important purpose of any Christian young person on a date should be to glorify God.

It doesn't work to try to glorify God on Sundays and leave Him home when you're on a date. When He comes into your life, He's there forever. If you can glorify God on a date, then you will be likely to do the same in other areas of your life. Isn't dating one of the thornier areas?

There are, of course, other purposes for dating, some on a very practical level. One is to have fellowship with members of the opposite sex. Too often in our boy-meets-girl culture, the sole purpose of dating is to find a boyfriend or girlfriend, go steady, and plan for marriage. But a strong case should be made, especially for Christians, for dating just for friendship and fellowship. Date to get to know members of the opposite sex. Men and women were created differently not only physically, but also mentally and emotionally.

1. The Opposite Sex Is Really Opposite

I have always found that women and girls tend to be much more emotionally sensitive than I am. If it were not for my wife, I could easily become a hard person. In talking with her, listening to her, learning from her, I realize how people react to words and actions and I try to be more sensitive.

On the other hand, there are areas in which she has learned a great deal from me. We complement each other. We need each other. It wouldn't hurt for me to have learned many of these things when I was younger, from a friend who just happened to be a girl. Certain areas of communication—especially love between the sexes—should be saved for that special someone you will marry someday. But wouldn't it be great to bring into that relationship a wealth of knowledge about practical things that you learned from a friend of the opposite sex?

Get to know several such friends. Someday you will probably date someone who appeals to you as no one else has, and the two of you will decide to spend the rest of your lives together. Don't enter that relationship without knowledge of how the opposite sex thinks and reacts. Enter it innocently in the area of sex and physical love, for that is what God intends for the most beautiful aspect of marriage. But there's no reason to be totally ignorant about the opposite sex.

2. Dating: Fun Without Fear

A second reason for dating is to have a good time. Christian young people, like most young people, usually have enthusiasm and energy. Adding the joy of the Lord to that (Nehemiah 8:10) should make Christians some of the most bubbly, fun-loving people around.

One reason I didn't become a Christian sooner

than I did was that all the Christians I knew looked like they'd been vaccinated with pickle juice. I thought that Christianity must be dull and drab to end up in such sour-looking faces. Once I came to know Christ, I found that He did as He promised: He gave peace and joy and abundance, direction and purpose.

Some people think the Christian life is a list of do's and don'ts, a drudgery. But I know from experience that life in Christ can be exciting and victorious.

The world says that the way to joy comes from outside. You have to have some *thing*: some booze, some dope, or some sex. But the joy of the Christian is not from outside; it's from within, from Christ living in us. God wants us to have a good time, to enjoy this life. He created us, put us here, and wants to live in us as Saviour and Lord and give us the fullest life of all.

A friend of mine once told me that he could have more fun sitting on a tree stump and reading his Bible for 15 minutes than he had at all the parties he'd ever been to with all the drinking, dancing, dope, and girls. When I first heard that, I thought he was crazy. But after I became a Christian, I knew what he meant.

Being with Christian friends and living in the Lord became far more satisfying than all the misfired attempts at peace and joy I had made while seeking what the world said was happiness. What a great message for the world: Our joy comes from within. Jesus said, "He who believes in Me, as the

Scripture said, 'From his innermost being shall
flow rivers of living water' " (John 7:38).

God is the Creator of life, the Giver of life, and
Life itself. When you have Christ in you, you have
the best portion of life. You can experience and
enjoy dates that are good times of fellowship in
Him.

3. How To Love Someone—Even If He's A Christian

A third purpose for dating is simply learning to
get along with other Christians and being able to
love them in the Lord. One of the biggest barriers
that keeps people from coming to Christ is the
sight of bickering Christians. They claim to love
the same Lord, yet they argue and fuss and can't
get along. Obviously, this is the opposite of what
Jesus had in mind when He said, "A new commandment I give to you, that you love one
another, even as I have loved you, that you also
love one another. By this all men will know that
you are My disciples, if you have love for one
another" (John 13:34-35).

Dating gives us an opportunity to love someone
else in Christian brotherhood. It's easy to love
someone you don't know. But it's different when
you get to know that someone personally and
realize that he has faults.

When my wife Tex and I were first dating, we
each thought the other one was perfect. I thought
she was the epitome of a girl who had never failed
God. The more we dated and got to know each

other, we learned about each other's faults, failures, and hang-ups, as well as good points.

When we married and began living together, this discovery time intensified and many little irritating things were magnified. Squeezing the toothpaste tube from the other end than your spouse seems like a nit-picky problem, but you'd be surprised how gigantic little things like this may become.

4. Learning To Accept The Hang-ups

Through a healthy dating relationship, you can learn more and more about a person and develop the habit of letting little irritations slip by or else talking them out. You will still have surprises should you two marry, but a fourth dating purpose is to develop a pattern of acceptance and forgiveness. Getting past infatuation to forgiving and accepting your loved one as human is one crucial thing you'll learn.

Again, this can be a testimony to God's love. The Bible says that God loves me in spite of myself (Romans 5:8). I'll tell you, that excites me. He commands us to love each other the same way, even when we learn of our loved one's shortcomings.

5. Getting Prepared For Marriage

A fifth purpose for dating is to prepare for marriage. Keep this in mind: You will probably marry one of the people you date. The Bible indicates that a man will "find a wife" (Proverbs 18:22), and in our culture that means he will search by dating. The Bible says this searching is good and will obtain favor from the Lord.

One of the greatest things about our marriage is that Tex and I tell each other what is on our minds. We talk about our dreams, our goals, our frustrations, and our failures. Many married couples don't communicate this way and their marriages are often headed for disaster. Tex and I began this intimacy when we dated.

By the time we were married, she knew of my dreams to serve God in a preaching ministry. And I knew what she wanted from her Christian walk as well. This set a direction for our marriage.

6. Dating And Spiritual Growth

One more purpose for dating is to help us grow spiritually. "Consider it all joy, my brethren, when you encounter various trials; knowing that the testing of your faith produces endurance. And let endurance have its perfect result, that you may be perfect and complete, lacking in nothing" (James 1:2-4). If the dating life isn't a parade ground for "various trials," I don't know what is! There is temptation, disappointment, and even failure. For a Christian, God can make this a tremendous experience of spiritual and mental growth.

I have a little boy and girl who gave us no end of delight as they learned to walk. They'd take a step and fall, and then they'd rub their heads or their rear ends and start off again. They fell often and there were many hurts and bumps and tears, but every time they got back up and took off. They grew, they learned, they developed, and now, of course, they can walk without falling very often.

The same is true in dating. Failure should bring growth. Trials and troubles will teach us to advance in spite of emotional bumps and bruises. Breakups seem like the end of the world, but time will prove that God can use such emotional setbacks to mature us. We truly grow when we learn to forgive. And there will be no end to the need to forgive, once you start dating. It seems everyone gets hurt at one time or another while dating.

Jesus wants us to forgive continually (Matthew 18:21-22). One of the greatest characteristics of our Lord was His ability to forgive even His arch enemies—those who had Him nailed to the cross. Before we were Christians, we *were* His arch enemies, yet He forgave us. The person who wants to be Christlike must learn to forgive as Christ forgave.

If you can see God's purpose in your dating, even in the hurts of broken relationships, you will be able to forgive infinitely. We should base our forgiving others on God's forgiveness of us.

3   Whom Should
   I Date?

Believe it or not, the Bible is specific about whom
we should or should not date. It's important at
this point to decide that we want to do it God's
way. The guidelines are in Scripture if we want
them.

There are four main types of people you could
date: (1) a non-Christian, (2) a Christian who is
not living for the Lord, (3) a married person,
Christian or not and (4) a Christian who is in
fellowship with God.

The key to the guidelines in this chapter on
dating is found in the Bible, and the following
passage is one that hardly needs to be explained.
You can probably draw correct conclusions just by
reading it carefully. "Don't be teamed with those
who do not love the Lord, for what do the people
of God have in common with the people of sin?
How can light live with darkness? And what har-
mony can there be between Christ and the devil?
How can a Christian be a partner with one who
doesn't believe?" (2 Corinthians 6:14-15, LB)

1. Non-Christians Trip Over Their "Selves"

You can see two principles of life set forth in these
verses. The first is that a Christian's whole life
should be centered around Christ. The problem
with a person who does not know Christ is the
"self" factor. Life is centered around self: "I want
to do my thing. I've got my own thing going. I'm
doin' OK."

The Christian knows he can't make it on his
own. He needs Christ's power, love, and Spirit. To
date a non-Christian, he would have to seriously
compromise his philosophy of life. How can the two
of you be compatible when your outlooks on life
come from completely different places?

I've seen many Christian young people tube out
over this issue. They live for the Lord, only to
start dating a non-Christian and quickly have
cold water dumped all over their faith. The decision to stay with God's standard was either never
made or was forgotten in the shuffle.

We should be careful to realize, however, that
we are not licensed to think we are superior to
non-Christians. The point is to be careful that you
only get close to a person you could potentially
marry. A non-Christian is off limits in that sense
because you may find yourself compromising your
entire philosophy of life. My own experience on
the blind date could have been a prime example.
What if I had not prayed and dedicated the date to
the Lord? That would have set the tone for the
entire evening and I probably would have been

less expressive in my reactions to the good news of the organist who received Jesus.

My date would have wondered exactly where I stood on it all, and it's possible she would not have received Christ.

A friend recently phoned to tell me of his disillusionment with his marriage. He had felt a distinct call to the ministry, but his life was hampered by his marriage to a non-Christian girl. He had begun compromising his beliefs when he was dating, and he wound up falling in love and justifying his marriage. His ministry and his marriage would never mix and he missed out on a great opportunity to serve Christ.

2. Dating Turned-off Christians

Now, what about dating a Christian who is out of fellowship with God? Absolutely not. As Paul wrote the Christians at Ephesus: "Do not participate in the unfruitful deeds of darkness, but instead even expose them" (Ephesians 5:11).

When I first became a Christian I had been dating a girl for a year who had claimed to be a Christian. We dated that long and yet I never saw any evidence of Christ in her life.

It became obvious that I could no longer date her. Our lives were in complete disagreement. I wanted to live for Jesus. She didn't, even though she claimed to know Christ as her Saviour.

It was tough for me to break up with her because we both felt we were in love. I knew our relationship would not please God, and that was first and foremost. We tried dating for a while, but I soon found myself doing the same things I did before I became a Christian. The time had come to make a complete break. As hard as we tried, we couldn't make it work. Because one of us was not fully committed, our relationship was dragging both of us down.

As soon as we officially broke up, I began to grow in Christ again. I learned something valuable—God had a plan for me and would use me as long as I abided by His principles. I would have missed out on the relationship I was to develop with Tex if I had continued in that doomed match.

What about dating a non-Christian or a backslidden Christian so that you can either witness to or help the person reestablish communion with God? There are several problems.

For one thing, it's easier for you to be pulled down to an ungodly level than for your date to be pulled up. It's too easy to become emotionally involved and even fall in love—then your good intentions quietly fall apart.

There is also a pattern problem. Dating a non-Christian in hopes that he or she will become a Christian can end in a marriage that's often frustrating to the Christian. Life-styles are affected, and the frustrations last a lifetime.

It's easy for wrong motives to crop up in such a relationship. Often the will of God is not the issue, but rather, "I really like him or her."

When I told my girlfriend that we had to break

up, she cried and begged me to give our relationship one more chance. She said, "Oh, Sammy, I
know it'll work out. I'll live for the Lord, and I'll
do anything you want me to do. Can't we just give
it another try? I'll commit myself to God."

Without knowing the principles I now see in
Scripture, I received from God a small dose of
wisdom, causing me to propose a plan that
worked. I said, "OK, let's split up for two months
and not see each other at all. If you really want
God's will in your life more than you want me,
then you'll live for Him whether or not you have
me. If God's in it, He'll draw us back together."

I don't want it to appear that being away from
her was easy for me. In many ways, I wanted her
just as much as she wanted me. But having a first
love for Christ, I was determined to do what He
wanted.

During our two-month split, my girlfriend continued in her partying life-style. I knew then that
she had the wrong motives in wanting to stay
with me. She said she wanted to live for God, but
she had just wanted me. Her emotions had lied to
her and I think she really believed that her motive was right. But the trial separation showed
the truth.

God is interested in our motives. Wouldn't it be
terrible if you brought someone to a phony con-
version experience, based only on a desire to date
or marry you? The Bible is full of examples of
people doing the work of God for their own desires. (See the story of Abraham's promised son in

Genesis 16, out of whom would come the nation of Israel and the Messiah. Abraham became over-anxious and tried to have a child as soon as possible. His scheme backfired. A "false" child was not what God wanted.)

We as Christians have often produced "illegitimate" Christian children, because we have been so anxious to see someone come to Christ that we push them—through an emotional or physical appeal—to a "commitment" to Christ which is not real.

When I was leading a public worship service at the Democratic National Convention in Miami in 1972, I found that we were persecuted by people who had some sort of an evangelical or fundamental Christian background. They said, "Hey, we tried Christ and He didn't work."

What they were really saying, of course, was that someone had laid a heavy guilt trip on them—some strong emotional appeal that pressured them to receive Christ. They had made more of a commitment to a preacher or person than to Christ. And it didn't work. They ended up bitter and stood strongly against any Christian who came along.

Pressuring someone into receiving Christ just so he can date you is "missionary dating" and too often it ends in destruction. Of course, there are exceptions. But beware, because failure is the rule. The person who receives Christ should have a deep commitment to turn his life over to God.

If God leads you to be a witness to someone

through dating, go ahead and witness. Live a godly life before him. Encourage him spiritually. But if you become emotionally or romantically involved, you'll head for trouble. *God* will not lead you to date or fall in love with a person to whom you would be "unequally yoked."

3. Married People Make Lousy Dates

Not many young people are interested in dating a married person. But occasionally crushes develop. You may feel you are falling for a teacher, pastor, doctor, or an older man or woman. Nothing but tragedy can come of this, of course. Don't flirt or tease. Don't attempt what you think is innocent, light-hearted advance. A weak married person might assume too much, fall into temptation, and the whole thing could get bigger than both of you. Think of the potential for ruined lives.

4. Will The Real Date Please Stand Up?

The person you date should have certain characteristics as outlined in Scripture.

Your potential date should be Christ-centered (Galatians 2:20). When you're committed to Christ, you want His will rather than your own. Your dates should also have that desire.

One fruit of the Spirit listed in Galatians 5 is self-control, another characteristic to look for in your date. Paul writes, "Do you not know that your body is a temple of the Holy Spirit who is in you, whom you have from God, and that you are not your own? For you have been bought with a

price; therefore glorify God in your body"
(1 Corinthians 6:19-20).

A Christian's body is to be brought under the
control of the Holy Spirit. Each of us has sexual
desires. We can let them run wild and encourage
each other to do what we want, or we can present
our bodies to God as living sacrifices until the
proper time and place: the marriage bed.

Your date and potential partner should respect
you and your standard of conduct. Anyone who
says, "If you love me, you'll . . ." is not a person
who respects you. The Bible says that love "does
not act unbecomingly; it does not seek its own, is
not provoked, does not take into account a wrong
suffered" (1 Corinthians 13:5). The person who
loves you will not seek to satisfy only his own
desires.

There should be standards in any dating relationship. You need to establish how far you will
go, and you owe it to your date to say so clearly,
from the beginning. If he doesn't respect your
standards, he doesn't respect you. And how then
can he love you?

Another characteristic of a "qualified" date is
respect for parental authority. You may think this
limits your choice of dates, because you know too
few young people who respect their own parents,
let alone yours or anyone else's. You're right. Respect of parental authority is becoming rarer all
the time. But have you or have you not decided to
adopt God's standard? He is clear in Scripture on
the issue of respecting and obeying parents. (I will

cover this more completely in chapter 4.)

Those friends I ran into at my ten-year high school class reunion had no standards of conduct or communication on which to build their marriages. I was thankful to be there with my first and only wife, and to reflect on the patterns we established when we were dating—patterns that led to a victorious and growing marital relationship. My friends may think they've had more fun than Tex and I have, but we're the ones reaping the benefits of purity, solidity, and the joy of a happy home. I'll take God's route any time.

4 Parents and Dating

A man in Texas decided that he wanted to be the first man his young teen-aged daughter dated. He took her out to one of the nicest places in town and treated her like a queen. He was courteous and pleasant, and they had a great time talking, laughing, eating, and just enjoying each other.

When they returned home, he thanked God for her and for their time together. Then he told her, "Honey, I took you out tonight to show you how you should be treated. You demand that anyone who takes you out treats you with the same respect and courtesy as the father who loves you. Expect it and compare how they treat you with how I treated you this evening."

Few fathers would do this, but still they are concerned. Even though most parents and teens basically love each other, dating can be miserable if their relationships are bad.

Where do parents fit in? "Children, obey your parents in the Lord, for this is right. Honor your father and mother (which is the first commandment with a promise), that it may be well with

you, and that you may live long on the earth"
(Ephesians 6:1-3). Interesting, isn't it, that the
first commandment that carried a promise with it
was to young people? That commandment was to
love our parents in the Lord. If we do that, we'll
have a long life.

Many people misunderstand this and think it
means that we are to obey our parents if *they* are
in the Lord. But it carries no *if*. The verse means
to obey your parents in the spirit of the Lord, in
the attitude of the Lord Himself. Jesus' relationship with His heavenly Father was an example of
what our relationships with our parents should be.
Jesus spent time with His Father and knew what
His Father expected of Him.

His priority was seeking His Father's will before He did anything or went anywhere. We get in
trouble if we don't do the same. I believe that
every young person should spend time with his
parents. You probably know many people who
grow up without really getting to know their parents. It's tragic. It may even be the parents' fault,
but it's still sad.

Your parents may have reasons for wanting you
home at a certain time or not dating a certain
person. They may assume you know the reasons
for their actions. They forget that you need to
know what makes them tick or what goes into
their logic. Don't nag or hound or whine—ask
them. Say that you sincerely want to know their
reasoning. Sometimes, if their reasoning is faulty,
they may even see it and apologize and work out a

compromise. You'll be surprised at how they respond when you talk as an adult with them.

Does it often seem that your parents don't even try to understand you? Let me ask this: Do you try to understand them? Until you have children (and please don't tune this out just because it has a when-I-was-your-age ring to it), it's nearly impossible to understand parental love. Some of their rantings and ravings are really the only way they know how to say, "Can't you see that we love you and care about you and are afraid for you? Can't you see that we have invested our whole lives into your welfare? We'd live and die for your future."

Parents usually won't say those words, and perhaps they don't even understand those emotions themselves. But that is what they probably feel deep down inside. They don't find it easy to understand why you challenge, disobey, or ignore them. Talk with them on an adult-to-adult level; draw them out. Let them get to know you as someone other than their little runny-nosed kid. Some people I know in their late twenties still have a close relationship with their parents, and they're envied by many who know about it.

You may think that you can't talk with your parents. Start slowly. Tell them that you know you haven't been perfect and that you may have even failed them as a son or daughter, but that you still want to be able to talk with them. Tell them you love them. It may be the hardest thing you have ever done unless you have been raised in a home where such openness is natural and encouraged. But the rewards are countless.

You may even find that you can develop a prayer relationship with your parents. That may seem really far-fetched when you aren't even communicating with them very well yet, but make that your aim. If you learn to be honest with them and pray for them, perhaps you can encourage them to pray with you. They may be as shocked at the suggestion as you were at first, but think of the future of such a relationship.

My wife and I have developed a pattern of praying with each other. It is particularly rewarding when we have had a disagreement. We pray specifically for the very things we disagree on. Normally it goes something like this: I'll pray, "Lord, I know she's wrong . . . " and she'll pray, "Lord, I know he's wrong . . . " But by the time we're through being honest with ourselves and with God and have really reached out to touch Him, we are in each other's arms asking for forgiveness and insisting "No, really, I was wrong." The most important ingredient of that kind of prayer is honesty: Telling God, "though I know he is wrong, help me to be open. And if I am wrong, show me." Often both of us are wrong.

It's easy to get into hassles with parents about dating, but don't rebel. Set a specific time when you can sit and ask questions about where they stand on certain things. It may be embarrassing at first, but a regular time of getting to know each other can help eliminate heated arguments and surprise edicts.

We should obey our parents in the same spirit that Christ obeyed His heavenly Father—joyously. I can't see Christ moping around with a long face, shuffling and kicking the dirt and grumbling, "Oh, brother. My Father told me to feed those multitudes, and look at them! There are thousands of people out there and I've been preaching all day and telling them all I know! Now here it is nighttime and I'm tired. And now He wants me to feed them? And with what? Fish and bread. Well, I guess I have to do it, but I don't have to like it!"

That sounds stupid, doesn't it? I didn't intend to be disrespectful, but isn't that the way we obey all too often? If we want to be Christlike, we will obey joyfully, trusting that our parents have our best interests at heart—even when they seem wrong.

The Bible says that Jesus endured even the cross for the joy that was set before Him. If your parents set limitations on you, see it as an opportunity to obey the Lord and do His will. If you rebel, you'll have a miserable atmosphere in your home. Respond joyfully and you'll surprise them as much as you please them.

Don't ask, *How can I serve God?* Serve Him by obeying your parents—with joy. At home.

Jesus obeyed His Father immediately. Can you imagine Him saying, "Father, I don't want to heal that blind man. What if it doesn't take? Can I wait till the crowds are gone, or till evening?" I can't imagine God ever having to tell Jesus to do anything twice. As He got orders from His Father, He carried them out. Instant obedience. Not "just a minute," but right now. Obey now, question later.

In Jesus' relationship with His Father, there were things He didn't understand or didn't want to do. Jesus admitted that He would have preferred another way to save men than by His own death on the cross. But He said, "Nevertheless, not My will, but Thine be done." His wish did not get in the way of His obedience to His Father.

There are definite advantages to obeying your parents. The Bible indicates that parents are a spiritual covering for their children, to protect them from the devil's dirty tricks. The Bible says that Christ is the head of every man and that the man is the head of the wife, and the parents are the head of the children (1 Corinthians 11). This doesn't have anything to do with superiority, but with authority. As you obey your parents, they become a covering for you and can make decisions for you in wisdom.

When Should I Start Dating?

One of the best ways to know exactly when you should start dating is to ask your parents. Being human, they will probably spot your faults quicker than their own, but this isn't so bad. You are the same way. While you can't see your own immaturity or weaknesses, they can. They may decide that you should wait a year before dating.

Your parents are in a good position to judge your maturity in a physical and psychological context. Look to them for decisions, perhaps in consultation with you, on whom to date, where to go, how late to stay out, and so on.

If you're in submission to them, you'll find them valuable and protective. Rebellion is the attitude of Satan himself (see Isaiah 14). He was cast out of heaven, basically due to his rebellion against God's authority. The devil was into a philosophy of "*I* will . . . " He wanted everything his way. Dump that attitude quickly.

It's impossible to effectively tell others about Christ while rebelling at home. You may be saying the right words when you talk to people, but your heart and your actions are not in the right place in God's sight. Paul wrote to Timothy that disobedience to parents is one of the characteristics of evil men in the last days (2 Timothy 3:2). Again, rebellion is a dangerous course for any Christian, especially a young person in a dating decision. Break off with anyone who would encourage you to do something behind your parents' backs. Such a person acts in the spirit of Satan. That may sound strong, but the Bible says that the spirit of rebellion is the spirit of Antichrist.

All authority in heaven and on earth has been given to Jesus (Matthew 28:18). However, He has delegated His authority to your parents. Wherever you go and whatever you do, you will be in submission to some people and in authority over others. You'll be in submission to your pastor, your parents, your boss, and even to your husband or wife (Ephesians 5:21). Set the pattern now in your dating life, submitting to God and to your parents, and your life will be headed in the right direction.

5   Where to Go and What to Do

Rather than giving you a list of good things to do and bad things to avoid, let me list a few principles so you can decide for yourself.

1. Obviously, whatever you do should glorify Christ. If you're a Christian, Christ is living in you. Wherever you go, Christ will be there with you. Whatever you do, He will do it with you.

I've asked many young people if they would do anything differently on their dates if their mothers or fathers were to come along. This always causes some snickering and the admission, "Well, uh, yes, there are a few things we'd change." It is a funny premise (no one wants his mother or father along on a date), but your Lord is coming along whether you want Him to or not. He'll not be left out. Is He enjoying Himself? Is He being glorified? Is He ashamed of where you are or what you're doing?

2. Try to leave a positive witness wherever you go. You can do many things that are not necessar-

ily wrong in themselves, except they might not leave the best witness. A few years ago, when we were visiting in Germany, we were approached in a laundromat by two Hungarians whose car had broken down. They needed a ride back to their hotel. We gave them a lift, and in the course of our conversation, we learned they were rock musicians performing at the local Noncommissioned Officers Club at the American military base. We in turn told them about ourselves and our ministry.

They invited us to hear them at the NCO club. I told them that as Christians, we would go only to share Christ—not just to go. They agreed to let us talk to the crowd during their breaks, so we went.

At the club they offered to buy us drinks as a token of their thanks for our help. This is a high compliment in Europe. But with all the American military men there, I knew our drinking wine would hurt our witness. Rightly or wrongly, most Americans think of Christians as nondrinkers. When a GI noticed us drinking Cokes during one of the breaks, he said to his friends, "These guys are for real." In that small gesture on our part, right or wrong wasn't the issue. Leaving a positive witness was.

We know Christianity is not based on a list of do's and don'ts but rather on a relationship with Jesus. The world wants to know what effect our faith has on the way we live. Sometimes we have to cater to what they *think* is Christian. This doesn't mean we should constantly be looking over our shoulders to see whom we're offending, but we should always be aware that we are representing Jesus.

3. Any place you go or anything you do that would hinder your spiritual growth or tear you down should be left alone. Paul, writing to Timothy, says, "Now flee from youthful lusts (to want something so badly is sinful), and pursue after righteousness, faith, love and peace, with those who call on the Lord from a pure heart" (2 Timothy 2:22). Notice that he says *flee*. Turn your back and run as fast as you can.

Why is it that two young people from the same cultural background can make commitments to Christ at the same time in the same meeting, but then one will grow stronger in his faith and the other will bomb out? Usually it is because one has not fled a temptation that has put a barrier between him and his Lord. Something is not surrendered, and Satan has a foothold. Pray, as Jesus taught His disciples to pray, that God will deliver you from all evil.

One of the first things I decided to flee from after becoming a Christian was dancing. Dances were a problem for me because of the temptation to lust. It was a big sacrifice for me, but I made a commitment not to go to any more dances.

After about two years, I began to rationalize. I decided that I could dance and still be committed to the Lord, as long as I told others about Him at the dances. The first dance I went to, I witnessed

100% of the time. I didn't dance at all, and I was proud of it. I thought I had proved something to myself, the devil, and my fellow Christians.

But each time I went to another dance, I found myself talking about Jesus less and less and dancing more. Finally I wasn't telling anyone about Jesus. I was dancing and lusting. My spiritual growth was at a standstill because I had compromised. I had to get right with God again and determine that, for me at least, dancing was off limits. I'm not saying that a person who can dance without lusting should not dance (though I'd like to meet him), but for me it was wrong.

4. Another thing to consider when you're deciding where to go and what to do is the effect it will have on your date's spiritual life. Perhaps you're thinking of a place or an activity that's not a problem for you. But what about your date? Paul told the Roman Christians, "For if because of food your brother is hurt, you are no longer walking according to love. Do not destroy with your food him for whom Christ died. Therefore do not let what is for you a good thing be spoken of as evil" (Romans 14:15-16).

I don't want to dwell just on dancing, but it is a good illustration of the differences between the way guys and girls react. Ask around and see if you can find a guy who will insist that he has never lusted while dancing. You'll find scores of girls who'll say so, but guys are turned on sexually by sight and sometimes just imagination.

Most girls are turned on by touch. That may be simplistic, but it has been substantiated by research. Many guys get into trouble because they assume girls think the same way they do. If a girl is wearing something provocative, the guy thinks she knows the effect it is having on him. He feels he's getting a come-on and he can react in one of two ways. He can make an advance, and be hurt by a rejection. Or he can be upset with the girl for "making him lust."

If he knew that most girls do not think like guys, he might be able to talk with her about what her dress or actions do to him. Most girls respond to such information first with disbelief. They might think the guy is perverted or always has sex on his mind. The first part is not true; the second might be. That's the way we're made. A girl who hears from a concerned guy that her dress or actions are unintentionally turning him on should work at correcting the situation. That doesn't mean wearing floor-length dresses or Army jackets; there are ways to remain attractive and appealing without looking like you're on the make.

A simple rule for dressing modestly is to wear clothes that do not draw attention to the sexual parts of your bodies. Girls should check the lowness of the neckline and the height of the hemline. Guys shouldn't wear super tight pants. That doesn't mean you can't dress sharp and look great. In fact, as a Christian, you should look as good as you can without being sensual.

Girls, if dancing is bad for your date, even if it's not bad for you, flee the situation for his sake. To knowingly cause a person to lust is as bad as lusting yourself. Take your date into consideration in all things, not just in dancing. The issue isn't dancing, but pleasing God, leaving a positive witness, helping your date grow spiritually, and staying away from temptation.

I've spent a lot of time on lust in this chapter, and I'll not apologize for it. Sin begins with lust, and dating is a platform for lust as much as anything else. Jesus Himself made the commandment against adultery even more difficult to follow when He said that even a man who has lusted in his heart has committed adultery (Matthew 5:27-28). There would be many today who would say that you can do whatever you want as long as you don't go all the way to intercourse. Jesus says it's not the physical act alone that matters but the problem of attitude—lust.

Sin begins from within and ends in death (James 1:15). Lust. Sin. Death. If you continually go to places that will cause you to lust, you'll find yourself in sin and the result will be the death of your spiritual life.

David committed a terrible sin. He killed a man so he could take his wife. But where did that sin begin? With lust. He saw her bathing and it eventually did him in.

"For all that is in the world, the lust of the flesh and the lust of the eyes and the boastful pride of life, is not from the Father, but is from the world"

(1 John 2:16). The devil tries to make us lust. The flesh is where you are tempted. And the world is the means by which the flesh is tempted. If you can remember this, you can "Resist the devil and he shall flee from you" (James 4:7). Before we ever go out on dates we should give ourselves to God and His will and flee the devil.

There are some things and some places that are spiritual suicides. Like a high bridge is a suicidal place for our bodies to be playing around on, so are some places bad news spiritually. If I jumped from a bridge to the water 200 feet below, I could change my mind halfway down and scream for God to save me, but the act would have already been committed. I would be past the point of no return. God could miraculously save me, but barring that, the impact alone would probably kill me.

That's like a couple going to a place that breeds lust, and later parking or going to an empty house or apartment. One thing leads to another. Then in the middle of the action, they want to cry out and pray that God will not let them go all the way. But it's too late. The praying should have been done long before, long enough before so they would not even go to places that cause lust or to unchaperoned spots were sexual activity can go unchecked.

The flesh means our bodies, our minds, our emotions. This is where Satan attacks us, using things in the world. To combat the flesh, we must set up standards. Christianity is not a list of standards, but there is merit in setting up our own rules to keep us in tune with God.

We want to make the best of our lives by using common sense. I don't want to sound like an ancient parent, but let me share some specifics with you for your own protection. Adapt them as necessary. Things I would frankly counsel against on any date would be the following: caressing of erogenous zones (these differ with individuals, but the basics are well known—legs, breasts, genitals); kissing in areas that really excite sexually; unzipping, unbuttoning, unsnapping, or pulling up or down on clothing. These should be absolutes, clear in each person's heart before he goes out.

Say to yourself, *This is as far as I will go*, and make it absolute. Even the world has standards for a woman who wants to guard against getting pregnant. Often an unsaved father will crudely counsel his daughter: "Do what you want, but if you keep your clothes on, you can't get pregnant." That's true, of course, but Christian standards are much higher than that.

Think of the reason you are kissing and hugging in the first place. Are all the hugs and kisses simply to show affection, or to give the other person a good time? If you get your date so sexually excited that he or she is frustrated unless there is an orgasm, what kind of a good time is that? And if it does lead to an orgasm, even short of intercourse, it's long past the point of simply showing affection. You're into sexual foreplay which is exciting, dramatic, necessary, and beautiful in the marriage bed. On a date, it will make everything else you have ever done seem like child's play, and the good clean fun you used to have will go out the window as you pick up where you left off each time.

There are many places you can go and things you can do for a great wholesome time. School activities, athletic events, and church socials are good if they don't conflict with the standards you have set up in Christ. Seek constructive places to go and things to do. Once a group of friends and I took our dates to a little church out in Louisiana bayou country for a revival. We had a fantastic time just being together.

Maybe you're not an evangelist, but there are many activities that can be more than just a good time. They can be times of spiritual growing and seeing God work. Remember, your joy is to come from inside you, not from the world around you. If the things you do don't seem as exciting or as sensual as the things the world does, rest in the joy that comes from being a Christian. Save your exciting sexual activity for your marriage partner. You'll never regret it, and you'll never have to confess to your husband or wife that you have done "almost everything" with someone else before.

Paul told the Romans, "Let us behave properly as in the day, not in carousing and drunkenness, not in sexual promiscuity and sensuality, not in strife and jealousy. But put on the Lord Jesus

Christ, and make no provision for the flesh in regard to its lusts" (Romans 13:13-14).

Leave no place for the flesh to take control.

6 Going Steady

Going steady is one of the most controversial areas in dating. In the previous chapters I've tried to state specifically what the Bible says and nothing else. It's difficult to do this on the subject of going steady because the Bible doesn't speak about it directly.

Young people go steady for many reasons, and there are many problems to deal with in going steady. After we have discussed them here, decide for yourself whether your reasons for going steady are valid and whether or not you are mature enough spiritually, mentally, and physically to handle it. Is it of God or not? Check the following warnings and characteristics:

1. One reason people go steady is for the security of knowing that they have someone who loves them. Perhaps their home life is insecure. Maybe the girl is looking for a father figure, or the guy is looking for a mother figure. Emotional stability is the benefit they subconsciously seek.

2. Going steady is insurance against not having a date for every event that comes along. The girl doesn't need to wait by the phone, and the guy doesn't have to worry about being turned down. And each date doesn't carry with it those "first time" blues: What will he or she think?

3. Opportunities for sexual activity always increase when a couple sees each other regularly. A friend of mine, before he was a Christian, went steady with 19 different girls at 19 different times. He knew that once he was around a girl long enough, and once they had progressed sexually to a certain point, she would be more willing to let him do what he wanted. He never dated around. When one relationship ended, he started another and quickly asked the girl to be his "steady."

Sex just for the purpose of sex is gross. Most everyone agrees on this. But some go on to say that sex with a person you truly love and whom you intend to marry is perfectly all right. That is contrary to Scripture. But many Christians have fallen into that trap. With the prevailing attitude, many young people go steady so they can engage in sexual play without the stigma of running around with a bunch of different dates. As we discussed in the last chapter, this is playing with fire.

My "19-steadies" friend often dated girls with great reputations. He was patient and waited until they were ready to loosen their standards a bit.

4. A fourth reason for going steady, and this is a legitimate one, is simply that you like being with your steady more than anyone else. He or she is special. You may be in love or on the verge of it, and therefore, I would recommend it to older couples. When you are in love, it is only natural that you will exclude all others, but if you do this at 14, 15, 16, the odds are great that you will get terribly burned.

5. Habit. You date someone two or three times and the word gets around that you are "a couple." This can be difficult, strained, and awkward for both of you, but it evolves. Emotions begin to take over, and though you can't get out of it, neither of you may feel true love for the other.

The only valid reason, in my opinion, for going steady, is the fourth one. It is a first step toward engagement and with it should come the promise of true love. It is short of engagement perhaps because you are still too new to each other to be making any lifetime commitments. You may trade rings or have a pre-engagement pearl ring or pin, but you are holding open the option of breaking up before you are engaged, or worse, married. And while it seems painful, I encourage keeping that option open as long as possible. As devastating as it may be to break up with someone you feel you have loved and with whom you have dreamed of spending your life, it is infinitely better to break up at the steady stage than the engagement stage, and at the engagement stage than after you're married (which the Bible all but forbids).

It's Good To Be Unsteady

There are reasons, of course, *not* to go steady. Only people who are mature in Christ can deal with some of the problems that arise. An old adage says you're only young once. As a matter of fact, you'll probably have the opportunity to meet members of the opposite sex for dating purposes during only one brief period in your life. There is no stigma about dating many people when you're young. And you're at a particularly sensitive age to learn from many people.

A counselor once told me that all of the things he learned in school about his ministry could be put on one sheet of paper. But the people he met taught him immeasurably. This is your advantage in dating several people.

Too often we tend to click and clique with people just like us and then we don't learn very much about other people. When you're not going steady, you're free to learn. No matter how much I disagree with somebody doctrinally or morally, if that person is a brother or sister in Christ and truly knows the Lord, I'll bombard him or her with questions so I can learn to be a better Christian.

Never turn down an opportunity to learn, and don't limit yourself to a steady unless you are near engagement age and believe that you are in love. The fact that you have already limited yourself by God's standard to date only Christians says that you can learn much from several friends.

Going steady often leads to a progression of intimacy. The more involved you become sexually (and this is normal, of course), the more you have to guard against lust and going too far. Familiarity can be a problem, and maturity is needed to handle such temptations.

Breaking up is one of the toughest problems in going steady. Some suffer for months—even years—and quit talking to each other. A breakup among lovers can literally split a youth group and hinder the witness and ministry in the church. Many emotional ties are built and when the dating relationship begins to falter, everything else is left in ruin as well. The insecure partner may beg and beg to stay together, but if you know you're not in the will of God, you must break it off, painful as it may be. Tact is terribly important in breaking up. Firmness without being blunt is the key—no walking out, disappearing, dumping, accusing, or surprising.

Another problem with going steady is that we often take on the characteristics of the people with whom we closely associate. We become like carbon copies of each other. Ruth Bell Graham, evangelist Billy's wife, in admitting their differences says, "If two people always agree, one of them is unnecessary."

If our steady has bad traits, we can often pick them up. We know our steady won't hassle us for being critical if he himself is critical. Attitudes and habits are garnered subconsciously.

Steady dating can make the relationship commonplace. You should never take your date for granted, but going steady makes it hard not to. There is no more calling a week in advance to make sure she's available. And there is less complimenting him on how he looks. It's a bad pattern for marriage and many homes break up over that problem.

Continually treat each other like king and queen, regardless of how steady your relationship is.

Young people who are not mature enough to handle going steady may find it an educational handicap. They get so wrapped up in each other that their studies fall off and their grades nose dive. This, of course, can jeopardize their futures.

If they look to each other for their security rather than to the Lord, they are in precarious positions. Resting in the promise of a human being is an invitation to disappointment. God will never fail us. When our steady relationships break up, we may blame God for letting us down. But if our trust is in Him, we can survive these disappointments and carry on in the Lord. Here again, we have a scriptural lesson: "Thus says the Lord, 'Cursed is the man who trusts in mankind and makes flesh his strength, and whose heart turns away from the Lord. . . . Blessed is the man who trusts in the Lord and whose trust is the Lord'" (Jeremiah 17:5, 7).

This was Abraham's problem. God had promised him a son, Isaac. Can you imagine Abraham's excitement when Isaac was born? Perhaps Abraham forgot about the Giver and began to worship the gift. Could that be why God tested Abraham to see if he was willing to give up Isaac?

The point is, are you mature enough to handle what God may have for you? Are you ready to go steady? See what your parents have to say. Watch for the warning signals. If people who love the Lord and in whom you have confidence can't say that your steady date seems to be encouraging you, beware. If they see that you have withdrawn and have become ingrown and inhibited, take the hint. "Where there is no guidance, the people fall, but that in the abundance of counselors there is victory" (Proverbs 11:14). Don't be afraid of counsel. Go after it.

Outsiders may see things that you can't see because you're too close to the situation. Don't ask your best friend who will tell you what you want to hear. Go to someone who will tell you straight out.

Beware of possessiveness. We'll deal with this more in a later chapter, but if your relationship is of the Lord, you will not find yourself or your steady so possessive that the rest of your social life is choked off. You should be able to have other friends of the opposite sex. If you and your boyfriend have agreed not to date others, that is one thing and it should be honored as long as you agree. But there should be no childish fits if you talk and have fun with others.

There should be no withdrawing from the rest of the group into your own two-person world where no one else matters. If this happens, you can be sure your relationship is not of God.

A third warning sign is heavy petting—your sexual activity becoming uncontrollable. The Bible indicates that if you are burning with lust you should either marry or break up. If you are not ready for marriage, run from it. New resolves and resolutions are almost always futile—or fatal—in this area (ask around, you'll see).

7   But I Don't Date

One of the greatest fears of many Christian young people is finding themselves without dates if they maintain godly standards for their dating lives. There may be other reasons for no dates—maybe they feel they're not outgoing enough, popular, good-looking, or well-dressed. "No one ever asks me out" or "No one ever accepts when I ask" are a couple familiar reasons for not dating.

Is this a time to lower your standards and go out with anyone who asks, or to ask anyone you think might accept? Of course not.

Remember, dating is purely an American cultural tradition. Satan may try to deceive you into thinking that you'll never be happy unless you have a healthy dating life and get engaged and then married by a certain age. The world (and unfortunately many in the Christian world) pushes young people into dating early, setting up an agenda of progressions from dating to going steady to falling in love to getting engaged to marrying, having children, buying a house, and so on.

Paul told the Christians at Colossae to see to it that "no one takes you captive through philosophy and empty deception, according to the tradition of men, according to the elementary principles of the world, rather than according to Christ" (Colossians 2:8). That could have been written yesterday, it's so applicable! It's the world that tells us we have to have a date every weekend or every month or at least for every major school event.

What is Christ's philosophy on dating? Read Phillippians 4:11-13. Paul said he had learned to be content in whatever circumstances he found himself. He knew how to live humbly *or* prosperously in every circumstance. He learned the secret of being both filled and going hungry, "both of having abundance and suffering need" for he could do all things through Christ who gave him strength.

Every Christian needs to realize his contentment is not in what happens around him but in Jesus. It takes learning, dating or not, to be content in Christ. If you're dating, God may have something different for you, maybe even something better.

I've seen many young people get turned on to serving Jesus and get psyched up to win the world for Him. But when the first wave of problems smashed into the boat, when the first real rough water came, they mutinied. They needed everything to be just right or they couldn't handle it. Their walk with God was not strong; they were not mature. They looked to circumstances for their contentment.

Do you feel it would be tragic if God didn't give you a mate by the time you're 22 or 23 years old? Would you be in total frustration? Try reminding yourself daily of all the good things you have in Jesus. Who could need more? Sure you might want more from life: more external possessions or a wife or husband and some children. But if you don't get them, look what you still have—Jesus. Don't sing "Jesus is all the world to me," unless you mean it.

The Lord blessed me with a wonderful wife and two children, Paul David and Rachel Renee. God gave me many promises about my son, especially that He would use Davey for His glory. Imagine what raced through my mind when Davey began to choke on a piece of plastic one day. His arms and legs flailed and kicked and his face turned red.

Nothing we did could dislodge the plastic, and with little time to spare we rushed him to the hospital, racing the wrong way down one-way streets and praying that God would get us there in time.

On the way Davey's face turned blue as he gasped for air. I kept beating on his back and shaking him, but twice before we got to the hospital we were sure he had died. It was a horrifying experience that still bothers me to even think about. *God*, I prayed as we raced toward the hospital. *He's Yours. You gave him to me and if You*

want him to live, You will have to do something.
Praise the Lord, Davey was spared, and without
brain damage despite loss of air for several minutes. I believe I had to come to the point where I
was willing to give Davey back to God.

This is similar to the point we all must reach in
our lives. It's God who opens doors, works in our
lives, and gives us our looks and our personalities.
He made us as we are. He knows best, and we
need to be satisfied in that. If He gives you a boyfriend or girlfriend, be content. If He doesn't, be
content with that too. This probably sounds easier
said than done, but it's true.

When a pastor friend of mine asks his
parishoners how they're doing, they often reply,
"OK, under the circumstances."

He always shoots back, "*Under* the circumstances? What are you doing under there?
Live *in* the circumstances and *above* them! The
Bible says we're raised with Christ and seated in
heavenly places."

Paul had more to say about this when he wrote
to the Corinthians: "Yet I wish that all men were
even as I myself am. However, each man has his
own gift from God, one in this manner and
another in that. But I say to the unmarried and to
widows that it is good for them to remain even as I.
. . . But I want you to be free from concern. One
who is unmarried is concerned about the things of
the Lord, how he may please the Lord; but one
who is married is concerned about the things of
the world, how he may please his wife, and his

interests are divided. And the woman who is un-married, and the virgin, is concerned about the things of the Lord, that she may be holy both in body and spirit; but one who is married is con-cerned about the things of the world, that she may please her husband. And this I say for your own benefit; not to put a restraint on you, but to pro-mote what is seemly, and to secure undistracted devotion to the Lord" (1 Corinthians 7:7-8, 32-35).

Many people have misunderstood what Paul was teaching here. They think that he was a male chauvinist pig or was preaching that marriage is the pits. But his other writings (especially to the Ephesians) prove that he was a supporter of mar-riage and the home and family. He also, of course, encouraged men to love their wives as Christ loved the church.

Paul is simply saying that some people have a gift from God that allows them to serve Him while married, while others (and he certainly seems to include himself in this category) have the gift of celibacy—staying single. They can serve God without continually wishing they were married or without continually lusting and being distracted from their service to Him.

If a person is unmarried, in a totally practical sense, he is uninhibited in his efforts to serve God. Obviously, a married person has other respon-sibilities. But please don't assume that Paul is somehow suspicious of marriage. He calls it mys-terious and beautiful and reflective of God's rela-tionship with the church.

I frankly found it true in my own life that there was a lot more time to serve God when I was single than now that I am married and have a family. I am no less a servant of God now as a husband or father, but I sure find fewer hours in the day for the actual front-line warfare for the kingdom. To be the man God wants me to be, I must spend time with my wife and children. If I don't do that, my prayers will be hindered (1 Peter 3:7).

While you're young, and if you are not currently dating, don't feel that you're over the hill, have been put out to pasture, or destined to be an old maid or bachelor. You can be used of God now in ways that you may never be able to again. Use your time constructively and seek what God would have you do. If He has a date for you or even a marriage partner, He won't let you miss out. In fact, you may find your future mate in whatever line of ministry you are involved. (But don't let that become your motive for serving God. Too many young people go to church youth groups and even off to Bible college to "find a mate." If that happens, great. But that shouldn't be the purpose. Some kids even plan on being at college only a semester or two until they find a guy or girl and can drop out and get married.)

More people get in trouble over not having anything to do than over any other thing. If you're not dating, develop priorities for your time. Idle time can be dangerous. In Germany I told others about Christ in the prostitution district on Kaiser Strasse. I ran into a GI who told me he was already a Christian. He tried to tell me what the Lord had done in his life. "Well, then," I said, "what in the world are you doing down here on Kaiser?"

He said he was sitting in the barracks with nothing to do and the devil got to working on him and reminding him how nice it would be to have some action, and he went looking for it.

"Man, listen, if you've got time on your hands, we've got Bible studies at our place where you can really learn God's Word and you can do something constructive. This will keep you from temptation while helping you grow as a Christian at the same time."

You won't believe his reply: "Hey, I'd really love to do that, but the problem is that I'm so busy, man, I just don't have the time." I don't think he even realized what he had said. He had time to sit around and let Satan begin to tempt him, but no time for anything constructive.

Before I became a Christian I had been a leader in several youth organizations and clubs in the Baton Rouge area. When I became a Christian, I still had all those leadership qualities and enthusiasm, but now I wanted to use them for the Lord. My priorities changed and I wasn't so worried about lining up some action.

I wanted to do something more constructive for the Lord with my time. I called several of the area churches and organized what we called the Christian Youth Movement. We met every Saturday night and encouraged the young people to bring their friends and dates. Two friends of mine and I began to lead these sessions and we saw many young people receive Christ.

Just recently I returned to Baton Rouge to speak in a church and was surprised when I heard a local pastor say, "I became a Christian at one of the Christian Youth Movement meetings several years ago and was soon called to preach." To God be the glory! God used time that I had given Him while a teenager to reach a man who would become a pastor.

Also during that time, I went to every old folks home in town looking for one that would let us hold a service for the residents. We finally got one to agree and we held services there every Sunday afternoon. I didn't know much about the Bible yet, but God made me a speaker. I preached one sermon so many different ways that it was a wonder God could use it. But He did. What a contrast my Sunday afternoons were then compared with a few months before when I whiled away the hours with my girlfriend.

There are many other possibilities for constructive service to God. You may not know exactly what to do every minute, but isn't there a needy bus ministry, a youth ministry, a puppet ministry, or Bible studies? Get involved.

When our ministry was headquartered in Chicago we held weekly Bible studies for young people. Young people from the whole area flocked to them because they had nothing else to do. Many of these kids are now in full-time Christian service. If you really know of nothing you can involve yourself in, ask your pastor or youth leader. Tell him that you have time, and you want to use it for God.

Organize. Set priorities for your time. Number one, of course, should be a quiet time each day with God. If you don't have one, you will not be able to determine what God wants you to do. This is one of the most critical areas for every Christian. So don't feel bad if you find establishing a quiet time is difficult for you. It's difficult for everyone, but it is crucial. Learn to spend time alone with God. There are several books available on how to do it. God will direct you as to what you can do with your time, particularly if you have the extra time that comes with not dating.

Remember, you may never date. Paul probably was not married. Jesus Himself was not. Samson got in trouble when he fell for a woman who was not in God's will. Delilah really turned him on, yet their relationship was ungodly and he wound up having everything come crashing down around him.

Of course, there are also great biblical examples of how God used people who were married and had families (Abraham, Noah, and others). Each of us has a gift, and it is not horrible to stay single until you're 30. (Many Europeans think 30 is a terribly young age to start a family.) Neither is it horrible not to get married at all, if this is what God has planned for you. If He has singleness in mind for you and you rush frantically into marriage, the deep wounds may never heal.

The pressure on us to date is totally cultural. Seek instead what *God* would have you do.

8 How Do I Know If I'm in Love?

One of every three new marriages in the U.S. end in divorce, and only six of every 100 couples who have been married 20 years or more consider themselves happily married.

These tragic statistics are evidence that Americans have lost the concept of love. Secularism—a philosophy built on people and things rather than on God—leads to such emptiness. The Bible says that God is love (1 John 4:8). To know love, we must know God.

We have diluted the very meaning of the word. It's not unusual for me to say, "I love Kentucky Fried Chicken." I also love my wife, but isn't she an entirely different subject? She hopes so!

Our language has been so watered down that we can hardly define love anymore. The writers of Scripture used several words to illustrate the differences between brotherly love, sexual love, and godly, selfless love—the kind of love I want to discuss in this chapter.

Are you in love? Do you know what real love is? Take the time right now, and maybe every day this week, to read 1 Corinthians 13—the whole chapter. It's not a long chapter, but it contains some of the most meaningful information you will ever read. Let it sink in. Realize what a wonderful, unselfish, supernatural quality true love is. Even the non-Christian world recognizes the truth and beauty of this passage. It describes the kind of love God has for you if you are His child. It tells of love almost impossible to duplicate—indeed, impossible without God in us.

Based on 1 Corinthians 13—the love chapter—check yourself on seven points to see if you are truly in love:

1. **Respect.** Love doesn't act unbecomingly (1 Corinthians 13:5). True love from God will have a reverence about it. I respect my wife in a way that I respect few people because I believe that God chose her for me. Being chosen by God doesn't mean that we always agree with each other. But my respect for her keeps me from acting rotten toward her.

Guys, if you respect your girl, will you tell her that "If you really love me, you'll . . ."?

2. **Giving.** Characteristic of God's love is that He gives. He gave His only Son (John 3:16). I can't imagine that God is in heaven just weakly loving people in spite of their sin. No. His love is active. He reaches out and offers forgiveness by His very nature.

True biblical love is more than emotion. Too

many married couples think that love means going 50-50. But love doesn't work that way. If each is truly in love, he will give 100%. Love is not giving something and expecting something in return. Rather, love is selfishness for our *mate's* benefit.

My wife has an unusual problem. You've seen the world make fun (in cartoons and situation comedies) of men who are in constant fear that their wives will go out and blow all their money on things for herself. With Tex and me, the problem is that we hardly ever buy anything for ourselves. We have to guard against spending too much money on each other.

I love finding clothes that will look great on Tex and that will please her. It's funny at Christmastime when we "limit" how much we can spend on each other. She says, "That's not fair! If I can't spend any more than this on you, then you can't spend any more on me!"

This attitude carries over into all other areas of life too. Because of our love for each other, we try to please each other psychologically, physically, mentally, emotionally, and spiritually.

The couple that always argues over "he wants to do this but I want to do that" is made up of two people who are in love not with each other but with themselves.

3. **Responsibility.** Are you willing to take the responsibilities along with the privileges afforded you in a loving relationship? Paul told Timothy

that the person who does not provide for his own family has denied the faith and is worse than an unbeliever (1 Timothy 5:8). That's pretty strong, but that's what the Bible says.

The person who claims to be a Christian, yet acts ungodly by ignoring responsibility, is a hypocrite. Do you want sex without marriage? Marriage without work?

4. **Encouragement.** Love does not rejoice in unrighteousness, but in truth (1 Corinthians 13:6). Is your partner being dragged down spiritually? If you are really in love you will rejoice only when he or she is growing spiritually. According to this Scripture, a preacher who is active in a ministry, but neglects his family, does not love them. The kids see a perverted type of love and wind up rebelling against God.

A pattern of true love begins while dating when you begin praying that he or she will grow spiritually.

5. **Confidence.** Does your love produce confidence, or jealousy and possessiveness? One of the greatest problems I had in my early Christian life was that I wanted to slug anyone who even talked to my dates. The more I tried to fight that jealousy, the more jealous I became. Sometimes I wished that the Lord would turn His back so I could punch a guy just once! Two things helped me to overcome it. The first was realizing that only Christ could help me. The second was that I met a

girl, Tex, who really loved me. The jealousy melted away because she loved me in a way that gave me total confidence. It was a test that she enabled me to pass.

Only God could give her a love for me that no one else had ever expressed for me. That love has freed me to minister without worrying about her and whether or not she is faithful or still cares. That's God-given love. (By the same token, I have confidence in God's saving love. That's salvation: responding to God's love.)

6. **Forgiveness.** Love forgives. Jesus forgave even those who mocked Him, ridiculed Him, spit at Him, gambled for His garment, and nailed Him to the cross. Read verse 5 in the love chapter. If you can't forgive, you are not in love.

Once my wife and I went to bed in disagreement. That's unusual for us because we try to clear the air, as Scripture teaches ("let not the sun go down upon your wrath"). I don't remember the issue, but I do remember that I was right and my wife was wrong; therefore, she'd wronged me.

I lay back on the pillow confident that I was right, but it was Tex who dropped immediately off to sleep. She was resting in the peace of God and I was tossing and turning until I could hardly stand it. Finally I protested to God.

It's not fair, is it? I prayed. *I'm right, she's wrong, but I'm disturbed and she's sleeping.* God impressed heavily upon me that I was not in His will. He made it clear to me that the issue was not rightness and wrongness but forgiveness. If I had really been wronged, I was not to take it into account. Rather, to be in God's will, I was to love her as Christ loved the church.

I woke her up to apologize and ask her forgiveness. Only then could I sleep.

Again, this is a pattern that must start when you are dating. How potentially disastrous to go into a marriage with a list of things in the back of your mind for which you have never really forgiven your partner. Clear them away daily.

7. **Understanding and communication.** The New Testament indicates that if I don't grant my wife "honor as a fellow-heir of the grace of life," my prayers will be hindered (1 Peter 3:7).

Lack of honor for a partner will hinder communication and can spell the ruin of any relationship, even some of the longer and more established marriages. Tex and I still try to share our thoughts with each other at every point. Some of the things in my ministry have been unorthodox—even radical. This is often hard for her to understand, and she lets me know it sometimes. God wants me to honor this, to be sensitive to her feelings. I seek her opinion and if we disagree, I look for her to submit to my authority and trust me. And she does. Because we communicate.

When I've been wrong, God has touched me and has used her to help stop me from doing something before it is too late. And when I have been right, He has given her peace so that she can encourage me.

If lines of communication completely break down, you're not in love. Begin the pattern of communication now. An open line of communication in a marriage can be a great source of witness to an unbeliever. It's not unusual for a person to get his first glimpse of the love of God in the marriage of two people who truly care for each other.

Jesus told His disciples, "No longer do I call you slaves; for the slave does not know what his master is doing; but I have called you friends, for all things that I have heard from My Father I have made known to you" (John 15:15). They had entered into a new relationship with Him. A friendship.

True love also means friendship. My wife is my best friend. When I sense God leading me in a new direction or convicting me about certain areas of my life, I'll ask my wife to join me somewhere for a Coke and I'll tell her all about it. We just talk. She needs to know where I'm coming from, and I need her input.

Love is a response to the total individual. Paul described the *total* individual to the Thessalonians: "Now may the God of peace Himself sanctify you entirely; and may your spirit and soul and body be preserved complete, without blame at the coming of our Lord Jesus Christ" (1 Thessalonians 5:23).

We are three beings rolled into one: body, mind,

and spirit. I can't talk only to your mind and not to your body, or only to your body and not to your spirit. If you are in love with someone's body (and someday you should be) but not his mind and spirit, you are not truly in love. If the best thing you can say about your "loved" one is that he or she is "foxy," you're in trouble. True love engulfs the total person.

Test your love on this basis and see how it compares with the quality of God's love as set forth in Paul's love chapter. These are qualities that can grow in us as we mature. Look to them as models and you'll know whether or not you are really in love.

9 Does God Have a Special Person for Me?

Some people think it's stupid to believe that God has a special person picked out for each of us to marry. I disagree. I believe God has a specific plan and purpose for every individual, including *whether* he or she will marry. And for those who should marry, I believe God has a perfect will (including the right person) in mind.

Believing God picks our mate may appear stupid to some people. *If I happen to marry the wrong person, I'm out of God's will and have ruined my life*, they think. But that's not true. The Bible gives examples where men or women have missed God's perfect will but have been happy and prosperous in their marriages.

I haven't always been convinced of this, but as I've earnestly sought God's will in my life, I have become convinced that God is interested in the specifics of my future.

In college I became engaged to a girl who was as committed to Christ as I was. She was the first runner-up to Junior Miss Louisiana and told about her close relationship with God at the competition. We prayed together often, and things seemed to be going smoothly, but there was always something lacking in our relationship. We tested our love by the standards outlined in the previous chapters, but as soon as we were engaged, I lost the sense of peace I once had. God had been trying to tell me that He was not in our relationship, but I wouldn't listen. It didn't make sense to me when everything else seemed to be so right. I was so emotionally involved with thinking I loved her that I didn't want anything to rock the boat. I lost sight of the will of God.

It was difficult, but a couple of months before we were to have been married, I broke off the engagement. Deep down, we both knew it was God's will. A few months later I met Debra Ann Sirman, better known as Tex.

Looking back, I can see how God spared me a lot of heartache and heartbreak. I could have married the first girl (and she was a fantastic Christian) but it would have been nearly impossible for her to fit in with the type of ministry God called me to: traveling all over the world, sometimes sleeping in campers, going without luxuries and sometimes even many necessities. She would have, on the other hand, made a tremendous pastor's wife, a woman who would be a fantastic hostess.

Tex enjoys traveling and even roughing it at times, and we have been perfect for each other.

The first girl did marry a pastor, and they are perfect for each other as well. I can now see how big a mistake we almost made, and I praise God for not giving us peace till we broke our engagement. Remember, we felt we loved each other and our relationship was centered upon Christ. Still, it didn't fit into God's plan.

The world says that if you marry the wrong person, you simply get a divorce, go your separate ways, and that's the end of that. But our philosophy is not built on the world's standards. When a man and a woman say "I do" and commit their lives to each other, God makes a commitment to that relationship too. There is a tremendous depth of meaning behind commitments we make in the sight of God.

There are three great commitments that every person has to make eventually.

1. Who or what will control my life? As Christians, we are taught in Scripture that Jesus Christ wants to control our lives. Will Christ, or self, or circumstances, or an outside party control our lives?

2. What will be my purpose or direction in life? Exactly where am I going in my job, my life-style, and my surroundings? For the Christian, the question is, "What will God have me do?"

3. Shall I marry, and if so, with whom should I spend the rest of my life?

Settle on the first two before you seek to answer number three. Too many people head into number three with no preparation whatsoever. To find

God's perfect choice, you need to have made the decision that Christ will control your life and that you will head in the direction He leads. Then, when you look for number three, your potential mate must have the same Master and the same mission.

Now, how to find that person God has for you. "The steps of a man are established by the Lord; and He delights in his way" (Psalm 37:23). Commit your life to Him and let God establish your steps. Don't run ahead and make your own decision. He will bring people and circumstances into your life as He wants to. There may even be some disappointments and bitter failures, all in the plan of God for you. The perfect choice of a life's mate is worth the wait.

What should you give to the Lord first? Give Him your works. If you commit your works to the Lord, he will establish your plans. People always ask me how they should go about finding God's will in life's major decisions. I always ask: "Are you following His leading, His will, now, in boring things of life? Are you doing what you already know He would have you do?" That includes reading the Bible, sharing Christ with others, and praying. These are clearly taught in Scripture as the will of God. If you don't follow Him in these, you can't expect Him to drop a chunk of His will in your Easter basket when you look for your life's mate.

Think of God's will as a huge wall. The person and direction God has for you is clearly defined—on the other side of the wall. You can try to jump high enough to see over, but it would be easier to get a ladder and climb one step at a time till you can see over. If you've already given your works to the Lord, you're following Him step by step and He'll lead you to His will without a great deal of soul-searching and effort. You will have established a pattern and a habit of following Him daily.

Our God is a God of *now*. Moses asked Him, "If I am supposed to lead the Children of Israel out of bondage, who am I supposed to say sent me?"

God responded: "I am that I am." Not "I was that I was," or "I will be what I will be" (Exodus 3).

Jesus came close to being stoned several times because He would answer the scribes and the Pharisees simply with "I am." He's the God of right now, the God of the present tense. To find His will for the future, trust Him in the present. The present will become future, and you will be in the will of God.

The day will come when you can see over the wall and you will know God's plan for your life. How you will know for sure, I can't say. But you will know. How did I know it was Tex for me and not the girl I was first engaged to? Was it the unrest God gave me in the first relationship, or was it the peace he gave me when Tex and I considered marriage? Maybe both. But I just knew without any doubts or unrest. And that came from confidence in God.

Another way to be sure of God's plan for you is through His Word. "Establish my footsteps in Thy Word, and do not let any iniquity have dominion over me" (Psalm 119:133). Consistent study of the Bible is the way to find out what God wants to tell you. In the Old Testament, God spoke in many strange ways: Through a burning bush, through a donkey, and through handwriting on the wall. Today He's chosen to speak to us through His Son Jesus Christ. The Apostle John referred to Him, in the first chapter of his Gospel, as the Word.

If Jesus is the living Word of God and the Scriptures were written by those whose lives belonged to Him, the Bible is the written Word of God.

I'm not talking about the Bible as some spiritual Ouija board. You don't just open your Bible and let your eyes fall on a super spooky verse that will speak to your heart and you'll know the will of God. I'm not saying that that hasn't happened (in fact I've heard of people who have said that very thing has happened to them). But this is not the primary way in which God speaks. He asks you to search the Scriptures daily, not to go picking random verses from your Bible and hoping for the best.

He speaks to you as you have a regular, systematic Bible study, as you meditate on His Word. I would even recommend reading a chapter a day, picking out a verse to memorize and meditate upon. God will speak to your life and you will have given Him an opportunity to lead you.

Be careful about your motive for studying.

Don't study just for the answer to one of life's great questions. You might be tempted to quit studying once God has led you in a certain direction. Study the Word of God because you love Him and because He has commanded you to study it. Study to communicate with God and your revelations from Him will not be gigantic extravaganzas every six months, but simple day-to-day communication. What a wonderful way to live!

If you looked hard enough, you could find a verse to back any idea you've ever heard. But that isn't searching the Scripture to find the will of God out of love and duty. That's looking for Scripture out of context to use for our own means. Even Satan quoted Scripture to Jesus to tempt Him. And how did Jesus respond? He quoted it back, in its proper context.

God will give you a sense of peace about His plan. Paul told the Corinthian Christians (1 Corinthians 14:33) that God was not a God of confusion, but of peace. When there is confusion in your heart and life, something is wrong. Paul told the Colossians to let the peace of Christ rule in their hearts, "to which indeed you were called in one body; and be thankful" (3:15).

I was so caught up in my first engagement that emotionally I wanted to be married. Whenever I paused long enough to seek God in the matter, I had no peace. I kept trying to push His will away until I realized the marriage shouldn't happen.

Everything seemed right and seemed to be working out great, but there was no peace in my heart—only confusion. I didn't want to stop and listen to God. I filled my life with so much activity that all I could hear was my own emotional being, saying everything was OK. But that confusion and unrest would not go away.

God also uses everyday circumstances. "I know your deeds. Behold, I have put before you an open door which no one can shut, because you have a little power, and have kept My Word, and have not denied My name" (Revelation 3:8). Notice God's promise that He can bring about a circumstance that no one can change. We don't live by circumstances, but by faith in God. But when He is first in our lives, He'll work out circumstances for us. And who could change such a circumstance?

When I was engaged to the wrong girl, God began working in mysterious circumstantial ways. My father fell ill and I had to switch to a college closer to home to be near him and the family. And Tex, who would become my true love, was attending that school because her father was transferred into the area.

I met Tex even before she was a Christian. Because of the lives of the girls in her dorm, she received Christ and He even used her to let me know that I was not living totally for Him. Had my witness been the only one she ever saw, she might not have received Jesus Christ. I was inconsistent and rationalizing certain things in my life at that time, but the girls who lived around her were living totally for Him.

God put us together so that we might find His will for us.

All through Scripture, God teaches us to wait for Him to lead us. If your love stands the test of time, it is because it is the will of God, providing everything else we have discussed checks out too. Read Psalms 27:14 and 37:7. God has the right timing for you.

When Tex and I began to feel that we were right for each other, we decided to test it by time and distance. Based on what I had been through before, I wanted to be sure. I transferred back to my old school 150 miles away and decided to just be away from her for a time. If our love was strictly emotional, it would have wavered—it would have come and gone. But if it was of God, my love for her and her love for me would remain true. God is eternal. Love that He establishes will last.

Our love grew even deeper and as the semester progressed, I was assured by God that she was the girl I wanted to marry. Time and distance had no adverse effect on our love. I'm so thankful for that time we took to test the will of God.

Often a person is in God's plan for you, but your timing is off. You may find yourselves drawn apart, only to be brought back together months or even years later when God's timing is right.

I remember when God first began letting me know that I was to minister to people in communist countries. I was super anxious to go and begin my ministry. I told my church and friends about my plans; then I blasted full steam ahead in preparation. People tried to raise money for my trip by having car washes and so on, but when all the money was added together, we had less than $75. I didn't know what to do. I wondered if I had missed God's calling or had misinterpreted it in some way. That would have shaken me to the core, because the call had been so definitely of God.

I began to doubt the will of God, putting the money into an account and leaving it there. Four years later, God allowed me to spend many months in fruitful ministry behind the Iron Curtain. The will of God had been clear, but I had jumped ahead of His timing. What God has done in our ministry there is related in part in *God's Love in Action*, a Moody Press paperback, and more fully in *Three Behind the Curtain*, a Whitaker House paperback.

Be careful. God may give you the person He wants you to marry five or six years after you meet him or her. It's important that your works are committed and God establishes your plan. If you're reading and studying His Word, and praying, He'll eliminate the confusion, give you peace, and your decision will pass the test of time. Then it will be the time to make the move that God directs.

10 Will You Marry Me?

Before a guy proposes or a girl accepts (or vice versa) both should be 100% sure of God's leading, based on the principles in Chapter 9. The person who acts without knowing the will of God is foolish (Ephesians 5:17).

An even bigger problem is created by a couple who are afraid to admit they've made a mistake by becoming engaged. They don't want to become the talk of their church, class, or circle of friends by having everyone ask what happened and what went wrong. It may be one of the most embarrassing, difficult, and painful experiences of life. But when compared with the devastation of either a broken marriage or a marriage that is simply endured in agony, a broken engagement becomes a blessing.

If engagement wasn't designed to have a potential "out" in it for either party, no one would need to become engaged. He would just race into marriage. No one wants to break an engagement, and many couples are so deeply in love at the time of the proposal that they swear to each other, "If we get engaged, there will be no breaking it off." This is unfair. Engagement is a trial period that should be an event that shocks both parties into realizing that they are no longer just friends, dates, or lovers. They are in it for real now, and if either is not sure or has any doubt at all, it's time to split.

Once marriage has taken place, a breakup is evidence that God's law has been violated (either adultery has been committed or someone has decided to end the marriage without biblical grounds) and many lives and futures have been hurt.

The period of engagement is preparation for the greatest adjustment of your life. My life was so radically changed by marriage that God didn't even clearly spell out the ministry He had for me until I was married. I was no longer responsible only for myself. I no longer lived alone. It was a tremendous adjustment to make.

You'd be surprised at the number of couples who are madly in love for six months during the engagement, yet three weeks after they're married they seem to be hardly able to stand each other. They let little things get on their nerves. Rather than giving, they're always taking and they secretly wonder what they ever saw in each other in the first place.

Part of the reason for our marital success is that we prepared for the adjustment during our engagement period. There were three things that we needed to prepare for: "For this cause a man shall leave his father and his mother, and shall cleave to his wife; and they shall become one flesh" (Genesis 2:24). There is (1) the leaving of home and parents, (2) the forming of new loyalties, and (3) the two becoming one.

1. Leaving Home

One of the most important apron strings to cut is the financial tie. The responsibility for financing your new life should not be your parents'. It is yours. We all know of young couples who marry and then count on their parents for the big expenses: appliances, trips, emergencies. It is wonderful when parents are able to help out, and it may be difficult to talk them out of helping, because they remember how tough it was when they were starting out. But there are physical, psychological, and mental ties until the couple is financially independent, so this is something that you should plan for. If you haven't lined up financial resources and regular income that will make you independent, you may not be ready for marriage.

Marriage is a new, frightening, and adventuresome time. One of the major causes for divorce is a hassle over money. And it is not always a problem of just not having enough to satisfy one or the other's spending whims. Often it relates to the cutting of the dependence on parents. A man doesn't want to be insulted by being financed by his in-laws. And a woman may not want her husband to count on his own parents. For the first few years of marriage, there will be an adjustment in the level of life-style. There will be expenses you never dreamed of, many of them tremendous. It may mean fewer new clothes, less going out, and fewer luxuries. Be prepared. Is a less luxurious life-style really what you want?

Start off as free from debt as possible. Many couples are immediately in debt for furniture, their honeymoon, a car, and other items. This is a heavy load even for a couple that has been married a while and has gotten used to each other's idiosyncrasies. It's too big a load for the newly married to carry. They need time to get to know each other, to discover that each is human, to learn to forgive, and to communicate openly with each other. As much preparation as you may make during your engagement, there will still be surprises in store. Someone once said that you never really know someone until you have lived with him. How true. Why muddle the whole scene with the burden and pressure of a huge debt?

We live in a society where budgets are built on little plastic cards. Want something? Charge it. Want to go somewhere? Charge it. But remember, the only time it "saves" you money is right now. At the end of the month, you can't pay credit card bills with plastic. It takes cold cash, and if you haven't got it, you can't charge it this time.

There is nothing wrong with the correct use of credit cards, of course. They can be more convenient than cash, but as a safe rule, you should use credit cards as you would use a check. It should represent money that you already have. If you use a credit card in place of money that you're getting next payday, what happens when an emergency arises and that money is spent the day you get it? Then you make the smallest payment possible on your credit card bill and the balance becomes a debt for which you can pay 18% a year!

Credit cards can be good for buying something on sale now that won't be on sale when you have money later. But don't forget that you've made the purchase and that a portion of your money is unavailable for anything else. Credit is also important in the event of an emergency when you need a quick loan. If you have good credit (in other words, you keep on top of your payments), you are good for an extension of a certain amount of money from the credit company (depending on your salary and other debts). It would be good if you never had to borrow money from a credit company, but knowing that it's available is good.

During our engagement, Tex and I committed ourselves to getting out of debt. School bills were paid and other loans taken care of. When we were married, we were debt-free. We didn't have a lot of money or possessions, but at least we were solvent. We were free to do what God wanted us to and to go where He wanted us to. He still provides the money and it doesn't have to go to satisfy a long line of creditors before we can apply it to the work He has assigned us.

Friends may have had shiny new appliances and beautifully decorated apartments and homes, but we were debt-free and ready to build. It is not uncommon for a couple to be in debt from the day they were married until five or six years after their youngest child has graduated from high school or college. The debts are finally paid off, the man is making the kind of money he could have used when the kids were growing up, and he and his wife have a big empty house, are debt-free, and are getting too old to enjoy it.

No matter how great your parents are, or how wonderful they are as Christians, or how well you get along with them, they should not be your first landlords when you marry. The engagement period is the time to look for a place of your own. Something just for you, something you can afford. It may not be as nice (and probably won't be) a place as you were raised in (another adjustment), but this should never be brought before each other as an accusation. It is the price of being married and starting a life of your own and can be one of the most rewarding and fun times of your life. You'll look back with fondness on the memories of a place that might have been small and crummy, and you'll wonder how you ever could have handled it. And you'll remember that Jesus was the glue that kept you together and made the place a great home to look back on.

The biggest problem with living with parents is that there will be two authority figures in the same household. Who is the new wife to feel allegiance to? It sounds simple to say her new husband, of course. But think about it. What if they are living with her parents? Does she want a cold war begun because she sides with her husband on an issue? Or what if they are living with his parents? Can he make decisions for himself and his wife, or will he feel the tension when he knows his own parents would have decided otherwise?

Get your own place and spend the time adjusting to one another, not to a situation with two families in the same household. You might want to consider having the guy live in the new place a month before the marriage, to start fixing it up. Being alone with the girl there before the wedding should be off limits because the sex drive and temptation will never be as great as when you are that close to marriage and "it'll only be a few weeks anyway."

Both Tex and I had grown up in big homes where our parents had provided well for us. When we were married we rented an apartment that had a clear view from front door to back door, right through the bedroom! To say the least, at $45 a month it wasn't the lap of luxury. We had decided during our engagement that we would rather live alone in post-marriage poverty than with our parents, and that made it easier to accept when the time came.

Now, several years later, we have been able to build our own home and we have been blessed with many more material blessings than we had when we started.

In our culture, of course, the wedding is an exception to the rule of breaking away from the parents financially. This is the last major financial role the parents should take in the lives of their children, and most parents who are able are happy to do so. In fact, they might be insulted if they were not allowed to be financially involved in the wedding. Some young people don't want to put the entire burden on their parents. Whatever they work out with their parents, based on the couple's ability and wishes should be acceptable.

Until you are pronounced man and wife, your parents are still in authority and should be consulted and obeyed even to the details of the wedding. This shouldn't be allowed to get to ridiculous proportions, for a parent who would try to dominate the wedding plans is not displaying selfless love. By the same token, the couple should not make unnecessary or expensive demands. Much compromise will make for a tension-free wedding. And remember, the marriage is infinitely more important than the wedding.

Don't make a scene if your parents want to help out in small material ways after you're married. It's a blessing for them to stay involved, but try to talk frankly with them about avoiding any major purchase that carries with it some sort of an unwritten dependence on your part.

2. New Ties That Bind

Besides the forsaking of ties with parents and leaving home, there is the matter of "cleaving"—forming a lasting loyalty with your mate. Your actual life together as a husband and wife team has to be planned and discussed. Use the period of engagement to set priorities and goals and methods.

You're committed to each other, so discuss exactly what this means to each of you. Through prayer and Bible study and even writing many of these things down (and keeping them), decide on a direction your relationship should take. You might want to decide to do this each week of your married life.

When you make it a habit to pray and study Scripture together while you're engaged, you'll fall easily into the same pattern as newlyweds, and also as young parents when the time comes. This is where the priorities are most important. You will have many things you'll want to do, but you can only do so much. List them in order of importance of what you want to achieve physically, materially, financially, spiritually.

3. Becoming One Flesh

Don't overlook the third admonition in Genesis, that of becoming one flesh. It is only natural as the time for the wedding draws near that you will become more and more interested in giving yourselves completely to one another. There is a lot of talk in the world today about trial marriages and living together, but the Scripture still calls this fornication—sin. Save your physical union for the marriage bed as God intended and He will bless you for it and make it all the more beautiful and meaningful.

Why is marriage necessary? Every commitment that God calls us to is public. He says that we should confess Him before men so that He will confess us in heaven. The disciples were not called as secret agents. They were called to *publicly* confess Christ. A marriage is an announcement to God and the world that you want to be joined in His name to serve Him and love each other.

Saving sex for marriage is more than waiting on a physical act. It is waiting on the total commitment, the giving of yourselves to each other in every way.

11 Looking Forward to Marriage

The couple that has determined carefully that marriage is in God's perfect plan for them should begin studying what the marital relationship is all about.

There are many good books about the subject, and your pastor or teacher or counselor can probably direct you to the best ones. Meanwhile, let's look at some of the things you can expect from your future partner. (I should point out here that it is best *not* to begin dwelling on marriage till you're definitely at an age and a stage in your relationship where you can do something about it.)

If you are still in high school, or if you are in a college situation that will be badly affected if you marry, it's usually best to direct your thoughts and efforts to making your present relationship as healthy as possible—including getting your education out of the way (successfully)—rather than concentrating on a marriage that may be many months or years away. This causes only frustration and much more sexual temptation.

During your engagement, study what the role of each mate should be. Understand that God's army is different from man's army. In man's army there are ranks, a pecking order if you will, and each person of higher authority gives orders to the ones below him.

God's army is totally the opposite. There is no rank. The Apostle Paul told the Galatian Christians that "There is neither Jew nor Greek, there is neither slave nor free man, there is neither male nor female; for you are all one in Christ Jesus. And if you belong to Christ, then you are Abraham's offspring, heirs according to promise" (Galatians 3:28-29). No one is better, no one has a higher place.

Certainly there are separate roles, but the male and female are one in Christ Jesus. Unity. Paul told the Corinthians the same message in a little different way that may help illuminate it for us: "Those parts of the body that seem to be weaker are indispensable, and the parts that we think are less honorable we treat with special honor. And the parts that are unpresentable are treated with special modesty, while our presentable parts need no special treatment. But God has combined the members of the body and has given greater honor to the parts that lacked it, so that there should be no division in the body, but that its parts should have equal concern for each other" (1 Corinthians 12:22-25, NIV).

God gives honor on the parts we think aren't as good so that equality comes to the body. The same is true in a marriage. The correct relationship between husband and wife, in this matter of position and authority, is seen in the relationship Jesus had with His heavenly Father. Jesus was God, and always will be God (see John 1).

If you read the second chapter of Paul's letter to the Philippians, you'll see how he explains that Christ, though He is God, and does not consider that position something to grasp, was willing to humble Himself and become a man, even to the point of being obedient to His Father and dying on the cross. He submitted Himself to His Father, but it made Him no less God.

Neither's position was higher nor lower than the other. They were equal. Yet they had different roles. They were different because Christ submitted and limited Himself to a human form.

The Bible clearly instructs husbands to love their wives "as Christ so also loved the church and gave Himself up for her" (Ephesians 5:25). Obviously, that is an incredible example, yet there is comfort in knowing that a model exists. Want to know how you should love and treat your wife? Simply study how Christ loved His church.

The church owes its allegiance to its Founder and Leader, the Lord Jesus Christ. For a man to love his wife as Christ loved the church, he must become her leader, her head, and the head of his own home. Paul says, "This mystery is great; but I am speaking with reference to Christ and the church" (Ephesians 5:32).

Guys, if you are to be spiritual leaders of your

home and marriage, you must become the spiritual leader while you are engaged. Establish yourself as one who can be confidently followed by his intended mate in matters of prayer and Bible study and worship. Then you'll be able to base your marriage on biblical principles.

The man should usually be the initiator. That does not by any means imply that the woman should not pray and study and worship. But if these activities are always her idea, then the man is falling short in these areas and she is forced to take over.

The parallel with Christ is seen in many of our church activities. When the church runs ahead of God and plans a big program, we ask God to bless it. God wants to be the Initiator. Let Him lead, and then we can join forces and be used in what He is doing.

As Jesus Christ is my Protector (I am in Him and He is in me), I should protect my wife. Think of the comfort of knowing that you are protected by God. Picture yourself as a small circle. Inside your circle is an even smaller circle to represent the Holy Spirit, God in you. Now in a larger circle, encircling you, is Jesus. And in a larger circle, encircling the Holy Spirit and you and Jesus, is the Father—God.

Before Satan can ever get to you, he must go through the Father. If the Father gives him permission, he must then go through Jesus. If Jesus gives him permission, you are still left with the Holy Spirit in you to do spiritual battle against

Satan. He may be allowed to tempt you, but you will never be left completely without your godly defense.

As a Christian, you are in the safest place there is, simply because of your Protector.

In the physical, emotional, mental, and spiritual realms, the man should be the protector. This was one of the areas that I was not prepared for before marriage, and it became one of the toughest areas of adjustment for me.

Someone began playing practical jokes on us soon after we moved into our first apartment. They would call in the middle of the night and play loud music and make weird noises over the phone. Satan nearly got to me through fear. I was freaked out. I realized that I had always been protected before by my parents or a college dean, or someone. Now I was in charge, and I was scared.

It made me depend completely upon Christ. Only He can give us the courage and strength to be the protectors we should be. There was nothing much I could do about the harrassing calls, but battling fear was one giant step in my marriage anyway.

My Wife Isn't A Church

Now, how do we love our wives as Christ loved the church? One of the ways He loved the church was in a fresh way. I'm glad that Jesus didn't get tired of the church and begin taking it for granted. If he had, the songwriter never would have been able to write that phrase, "Every day with Jesus is sweeter than the day before."

Doesn't taking each other for granted happen in too many marriages? The honeymoon is exciting and fun, full of anticipation. The guy runs around and opens her car door, and carries her across the threshhold. She cooks a terrible meal and he tells her it's just great. The next morning before work he plants a five-minute kiss on her smacker. This is repeated for a few days or weeks, but let's check in on them a year later.

He reaches across her to push her car door open, walks into the house ahead of her, holding the door ajar behind him, tells her the dinner was "not too bad," and pecks her on the cheek on his way out the door the next morning.

Five years later he's out of the car and grumbling his way into the house before she knows what's happening. He slams the door, almost in her face, grumbles about the meal, and instead of kissing her, indicates that she ought to be cooking better by now. His love has waned. She's been taken for granted. Is this how Christ loves the church? The church is a couple of thousand years old, and we have really blown it as Christ's bride. Yet He still loves us.

The day will come when the head-over-heels, can't-help-myself kind of love will end. Then it will become your responsibility to love your wife by choice. And isn't that better than loving her because you can't help it? Ask God for a love for her that parallels His love for the church. Make love an act of the will. Don't panic when the passion seems gone, and don't feel guilty when you no longer have that need to always talk with her and be with her constantly.

Jesus also loved the church to the end—to death. He didn't bomb out and say, "Forget it Father, I see what's coming and I want out." The song says He could have called ten thousand angels, but He died alone, for you and me.

No matter how much you love the Lord and each other, you won't be immune to problems, adjustments, and hang-ups. The difference is that you have the great Problem Solver, you have the Hanger to hang your hang-ups on, you've got the Adjuster to adjust your adjustments. His name is Jesus Christ.

During your engagement, commit yourself to Christ and each other all the way to the end. No matter what. Jesus loves the church to the end. Guys come to me and say, "Wow, man, I thought I loved her, but I don't anymore." It doesn't wash, guys. God can give you a love for your wife through it all.

What is the wife's role? Paul writes, "Wives, be subject to your own husbands, as to the Lord. For the husband is the head of the wife, as Christ also is the head of the church, He Himself being the Saviour of the body. But as the church is subject to Christ, so also the wives ought to be to their husbands in everything" (Ephesians 5:22-24).

That word *subject* should not be taken in a negative context. It means simply "to stand

under," in God's order. You are not less or un-
equal, but God has His order. As Jesus stands
under His Father, you stand under your husband.
Is Jesus less than God? No. And neither are you
less than your husband.

The reasons? One is that being "under" is a
place of mental, emotional, spiritual, and physical
protection.

You should want your man to be the greatest
spiritual person he can be. Just as God's power
can only be expressed through the church when
we Christians are in submission to Him, God's
power can only be expressed through your boyfriend, or fiance, or husband when you place yourself in submission to him. Notice the Bible doesn't
say that he is to boss you. You are to submit
yourself. You can release God's power on yourself
and your husband and your home and family and
marriage as you submit.

Once when Tex and I were first married we
were telling others about Christ in a coffeehouse
in the French Quarter of New Orleans. I was
sharing Christ with a Jew who had separated
from his wife, was involved in the occult, and was
into drugs. He wasn't listening very well and kept
coming back with a jumble of intellectual
arguments—until Tex came over and stood beside
me, that is. She bowed her head and prayed silently for me.

Not only did this release in me even more power
from the Holy Spirit, but it also had a profound
impact on the listener. Within a few minutes he

had completed his arguments and was ready to receive Christ.

A year later we read in a Christian newspaper what he saw in Tex and me, "something that all my intellectual arguments couldn't combat. They had something in their marriage that I knew nothing about." He had told his wife, who took a couple of months to see if he was for real, and they were eventually reunited and she received Jesus. What a testimony to a godly marriage, and praise God, it's not unique.

12 How Do I Start Over?

After reading the first 11 chapters, maybe you're more discouraged than encouraged. You realize that you're already into many of the things I've advised, through Scripture, to avoid. You've already messed up, missed God's will, have established bad habits, perhaps have even lost your virginity.

Guilt can be one of the greatest problems in your dating relationships, especially as you near marrying age. One of every three hospital beds in this country is occupied by a person suffering from severe emotional stress. In many cases the stress is a result of guilt.

Guilt needs to be dealt with without explaining it away by saying "everybody had done it." It needs to be faced. Admitted. Confessed. Repented of. Dealt with at the cross of Jesus Christ. If you are a Christian, you can derive comfort from these verses: "The witness is this, that God has given us eternal life, and this life is in His Son. He who has the Son has the life; he who does not have the Son of God does not have the life. These things I have written to you who believe in the name of the Son of God, in order that you may know that you have eternal life" (1 John 5:11-13). If you are not a Christian, you know how to receive Jesus, and I encourage you to do so, on your own or with someone you trust. (For another look at becoming a Christian, see pages 13-16.)

The Bible says you can *know* that you are saved, forgiven, and on your way to eternal life with Him. There will be no wishing, no hoping, and no wondering. Your sin problem has been dealt with at the cross. Then, before you can ever live up to God's expectations, you must give your life completely to Him.

This isn't a matter of knowing *about* Him. I'm talking about knowing Him personally. If you know Jesus in your head but not in your heart, you're off by about 13 inches.

Once you know Jesus, you can claim the promise, "If we confess our sins, He is faithful and righteous to forgive us our sins and cleanse us from all unrighteousness" (1 John 1:9). Confession is important. The moment you feel lust for someone, you should let God know about it. Don't wait until you've lost it all to temptation. Tell God about it—now!

Then admit that you're wrong—and that's tough to do. Search the Word of God, and if it contradicts anything you plan to do, as good as it may sound, you need to admit that you're wrong. God's standard is right—always. I don't like to find out that I'm wrong, and when I find out, I don't like to admit it. But the Bible says that none of us is totally right.

My son, who is five and a half, often does things that displease me, as little boys will do. When I find out about it, he immediately goes into his sorry routine. "Oh, Daddy, I'm sorry. I'm so sorry!" But is he sorry? Was he sorry when I didn't know about his action? Or is he in trouble and trying to get out of a spanking?

After a couple has gone too far, they may cry out to God that they are sorry. Are they really? Or are they hoping that if they beg enough forgiveness, the girl won't be pregnant? They need to realize, regardless of the consequences of their actions, that they have been dreadfully wrong when measured against God's standard. They need to be willing to turn from their sin.

That willingness to get away from sin is a gigantic consideration. It's possible to start all over again. If you sit around crying that you've already failed God and there's no sense going on, you're headed nowhere. God has offered, even promised, forgiveness. Let God know about that sin, admit that you're wrong, and be willing to turn away from it. Then get back up and go again.

When Christ told him he could walk on the water, Peter stepped from the boat and began to walk. It was exciting until the wind blew and the waves slapped his legs and he remembered his physics lesson and decided that he ought to be sinking. Before he knew it, his faith was gone and he *was* sinking.

He cried out for the Lord to pull Him out of the water. And you can do the same. God will forgive you and cleanse your life. What a great word "cleanse" is. Think about it. You know what it means to clean something. And when it becomes cleansed, it's as good as new. "As far as the east is from the west, so far has He removed our transgressions from us" (Psalm 103:12). Man, that's what I call forgiveness.

It is as though the sin were never committed, as far as God is concerned. But how about as far as you're concerned? Scars may remain. Sin is serious. Though sin can be forgiven, we may have to deal with the scars. Let God heal the scars too. God can forgive a girl for becoming pregnant, or a guy for getting her pregnant, but there are still problems to be dealt with. The result of the sin cannot be swept under the rug, though the sin has been forgiven.

If God has forgiven me, why can't I forgive myself? If God has forgiven you, you have no right to hold a grudge against yourself. The sin has hurt God more than anyone else, yet He has forgiven you. You must choose to forgive yourself. When doubts and fears and pangs of guilt return, recognize that they are from Satan. He'll constantly accuse you. He'll report, in effect, to God, the specific sin you committed. But Jesus will plead your case and say that He died for that sin a long time ago. The Bible calls the devil "the accuser of the brethren," but if you've claimed the forgiveness of Jesus Christ, your case has already been thrown out of court.

You'll probably find the feeling nagging you that "You've blown it. You're no good. There's no hope for you. You can never be used of God. You can never count for God."

Please don't listen to those lies. Listen to God who says "Case dismissed. You're forgiven."

A Small Giant Step For God

Picking up the pieces means learning to serve God. If you've failed Him, you may have to deal with the scars and the consequences, though you have been forgiven and cleansed. But He will also give you the strength to stay away from future sin and to deal with those existing problems.

Remember it is God who cleanses. He takes sin away from you. You don't have the power to forsake sin—but God does. And if you end up with His power, as it is promised, and if you are willing to let Him take your life, you can forsake sin through Him.

Jesus overcame temptation without sin. He's the greatest overcomer ever. You can become an overcomer by trusting Him.

Now what about forgiving the other person? Maybe he took advantage of you, or she let her standards drop. Maybe the sin wasn't sexual but was the evidence of neglect: A breakup or lack of concern for your feelings. You've been hurt. How can you forgive?

Practice what Jesus taught: "Why do you look at the speck in your brother's eye, but do not notice the log that is in your own eye? Or how can you say to your brother, 'Let me take the speck out of your eye,' and behold, the log is in your own eye? You hypocrite, first take the log out of your own eye, and then you will see clearly enough to take the speck out of your brother's eye" (Matthew 7:3-4).

In other words, before you allow an unforgiving spirit to dominate you because of something someone did to you, pray, *God, judge me on what I've seen in that person.*

My son used to have a problem with stubbornness—you don't know what stubbornness is until you've seen him on a stubborn streak. One day I was asking God why Davey was so cotton pickin' stubborn. The Lord spoke to my heart. "Sammy, where do you think he learned it?"

Wow. Right between the eyes. God had to deal with my stubbornness before I was ready to help Davey deal with his.

Let God's forgiveness begin with you, and when you are cleansed, you can forgive anyone.

Forgiveness is Jesus' way. He is *The Man* of Forgiveness. Forgive others, if for no other reason than that it is an expression of the life of Christ. Don't hold any grudges or keep any month-long hurts hidden away. Forgive your brother or sister before expecting forgiveness from God.

If you forgive to glorify God you are apt to become an emotionally, mentally, and spiritually happy person. And you will be free to be the kind of person God wants you to be.